waffles

waffles

betty rosbottom

PHOTOGRAPHS BY SHERI GIBLIN

CHRONICLE BOOKS

SAN FRANCISCO

Library of Congress Cataloging-in-Publication Data available.

ISBN 0-8118-4842-6

Manufactured in China.

Design and typesetting by Elizabeth Van Itallie

Food stylist: Dan Becker

Prop stylist: Leigh Noe

Photographer's assistant: Selena Aument

10 9 8 7 6 5 4 3 2 1

Chronicle Books LLC

85 Second Street

San Francisco, California 94105

www.chroniclebooks.com

Boursin is a registered trademark of Société de la Fromagerie Boursin;

Brennan's is a registered trademark of The Ella, Adelaide, Dick & John Brennan Restaurants, Ltd.;

Grand Marnier is a registered trademark of Société des Produits Marnier-Lapostalle;

Kahlúa is a registered trademark of The Kahlúa Company;

Mister Mustard is a registered trademark of House of Herbs, Inc.;

Nutella is a registered trademark of Ferrero SpA;

Pepperidge Farm is a registered trademark of PF Brands, Inc.;

Tabasco is a registered trademark of McIlhenny Co.;

Thomas' is a registered trademark of Entenmann's Inc.

Page 2: Raised Belgian Waffles (page 57)

For my family—Ronny, Michael, Heidi, Edie, and Griffin—with love

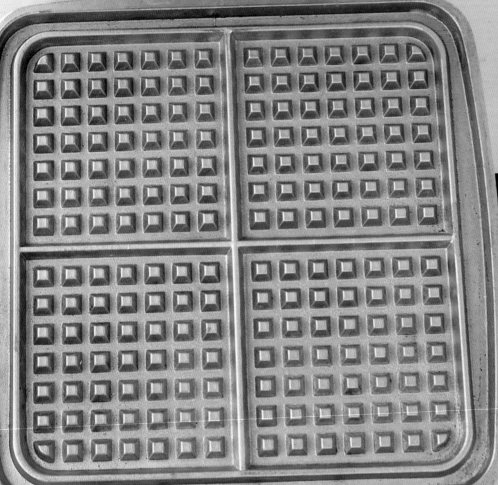

Acknowledgments

any thanks to my wonderful team of culinary assistants: Emily Bell, Sheri Lisak, Barbara O'Connor, Jane Giat, and most especially Deb Brown—who took care of so many details for this project.

I am indebted to the volunteers who tirelessly tested waffle recipes for months and then offered their critiques: Marilyn Dougherty, Jackie Murrill, Wendy Gabriel, Marilyn Cozad, and Ann Ryan-Small. My appreciation also goes to Jennifer Bourgeois, Brenda McDowell, and Neal Cavanaugh for helpful contributions.

Thanks to Ellen Ellis for reading the manuscript with her usual discerning eye.

A special hug to Sara Perry, fellow cook and dear friend, for so much encouragement.

To my talented editors, Leslie Jonath and Laurel Leigh, at Chronicle Books, I am grateful for helpful suggestions and wise counsel. Many thanks to photographer Sheri Giblin for bringing the recipes into vibrant color and to Elizabeth Van Itallie for her completely cute page designs.

To my agent, Judith Weber, thank you once again for your insight and guidance.

To my husband, Ron, who ate waffles from dawn to midnight day after day, almost without complaint, and to my son, Mike, my daughter-in-law, Heidi, and their future chefs, Edie and Griffin, thank you all for your love and support.

Table of Contents

Introduction

I can still see the shiny chrome waffle iron my mother pulled out for those special breakfasts where waffles were the star attraction. It didn't take her long to whip up a batter, which she then spread over the oiled grids of our waffle press. I would stand on the sidelines and watch until my mother lifted the lid and pulled out a crisp golden round. Then I raced to the table with my treasure and slathered it with butter and drenched it with maple syrup. I guess that's when my love affair with waffles began.

I, like many Americans, have long cherished my "waffled" memories, and thought of these baked honeycombed cakes as quintessential American breakfast fare. The truth is they neither originated in our country nor are they confined to the breakfast hour. Germans, cooking over hearths, made the earliest waffles back in the thirteenth century using hinged cast-iron plates attached to long handles to produce thin communion wafers. The French, Swedes, and Italians followed with their own adaptations. Immigrants brought waffles of all shapes and varieties to our shores, though Dutch settlers in the seventeenth century are credited with the earliest imports. Throughout the United States, waffles reflect the rich culinary heritage of these countries and many more.

Today's waffles can be either sweet, like those the Europeans arrived with, or they can be savory (definitely an American invention). And, no longer are waffles enjoyed exclusively as early morning entrées — we now savor them from dawn to dusk.

Waffles are winners on more than one front. They are quickly made; count on just a few minutes to assemble the batter and a few minutes more to bake. Many of the ingredients called for — flour, sugar, eggs, butter, and milk — are kitchen staples, so you can whip up a simple batch on a whim. For those cooks who love to make dishes in advance, waffles freeze well and can be reheated easily in a toaster or a warm oven. And, let's not forget the most important attribute of all — waffles are just irresistibly good. Biting into a hot waffle, crisp and golden outside and tender within, is like tasting a little bit of heaven!

Ingredients

All waffles have certain ingredients in common: fat, flour and/or grains, leavening, liquid, and eggs. Sweet waffles will include a sweetener, and savory ones will include salt and other seasonings. Butter, melted shortening, or vegetable oil typically provides the fat (which is usually on the high side) in waffle batter. Fat keeps the batter from sticking and makes waffles tender. Flours can include all-purpose, whole wheat, self-rising, and spelt; cornmeal, oats, or other grains and seeds are also possibilities. Milk is the most common liquid, and you can use whole, reduced fat, or skim with good results. Buttermilk, cream, yogurt, sour cream, and orange juice are other liquid alternatives

that can add richness and flavor to batters. Baking powder and soda are traditional leavening options, but yeast can also be called upon, as it often is in Belgian waffles. While white sugar is the most popular sweetener, light and dark brown sugars, and confectioners' sugar, as well as honey and molasses, are also choices.

Toppings

Toppings for waffles are like icings on cakes. On their own, waffles are good, but when dressed up with a special garnish, they are irresistible. Maple syrup and butter is the tried-and-true duo that accompanies most sweet breakfast waffles, but fresh berries dusted with confectioners' sugar, fruit sauces, and unusual syrups, plus flavored butters and whipped creams, are equally good adornments.

Savory waffles can be embellished just as creatively. Homemade salsas and fruit chutneys add pizzazz to such waffles, as do hollandaise or tantalizing cheese sauces. Fresh figs and goat cheese or sliced prosciutto and poached eggs make other dynamite topping combos.

Dessert waffles offer the greatest possibility when it comes to garnishes. They are delicious served with scoops of velvety smooth ice cream and with generous drizzles of warm dessert sauces. Toasted nuts and

WAFFLE TIPS

➤ Preheat the waffle iron according to the manufacturer's directions.

➤ Most waffle irons today have nonstick surfaces, but if yours doesn't, butter or oil it for the first or second waffles. After that, you probably will not need to grease the iron.

➤ If your waffle iron has a setting, set it on medium-high for crispy waffles or follow the manufacturer's directions.

➤ Waffle yields can vary depending on the size of your iron. The recipes in this book will give a yield indicating the least number that the batter will make. You may find that you have leftover batter. Bake extra waffles with the batter and freeze them for future use.

➤ The amount of batter needed to fill waffle irons will differ. Six-and-one-half-inch round irons, for example, need about one-half cup, while a large waffle maker will need more. Check the owner's manual for suggested amounts.

➤ Once the batter has been poured into a waffle iron, do not open it for at least 90 seconds. Do not try to force the lid open if it resists, as this indicates that the waffle is not finished cooking.

➤ Waffle irons differ in the amount of time they take to cook batters. If, even after the *cooked* signal has been given, your waffles are not as crisp or done on the outside as you would like, cook them a minute or two more, watching carefully. A general rule is that waffles are done when the steaming stops and the waffle iron can be opened easily.

➤ To remove cooked waffles from the iron, gently spear them with a fork or use wooden tongs and lift off.

➤ Keep cooked waffles warm in a 200°F oven. Put the waffles directly on oven racks. Do not stack waffles or they will become soggy.

coconut flakes, fresh berries, sliced fruits, and flavored whipped creams offer inspiration for "gilding the lily" when it comes to waffle desserts.

Toppings suggestions are included with each waffle recipe. Or, see the chart on page 93 for a comprehensive list of waffle and topping pairings.

Kitchen Equipment

WAFFLE IRONS: Waffle irons come in all shapes. You'll find round, square, or rectangular irons, and even some with heart- or animal-shaped grids. Belgian waffle irons have deeper grids than classic irons, resulting in taller waffles with deeper pockets. Some irons are simple and modestly priced, while those loaded with extras have higher tickets. Pick according to your needs and budget. When buying a new iron, it's important to consider which features you will use. For example, most waffle irons today come with non-stick surfaces, an invaluable aid. These irons work so efficiently that you no longer have to worry about batter sticking to the grids. Most irons also include a colored button or sound a noise to let you know when the machine is hot enough for the batter to be poured in. Many irons also signal when the waffles are ready. These features contribute to carefree cooking and help take the guesswork out of waffle making.

BOWLS: You'll need a large bowl for mixing dry ingredients and a medium bowl (or a large two- to

---

MAKING WAFFLES AHEAD OR FREEZING THEM

➤ Waffles are a great convenience food and can be prepared in advance and reheated with great results. Use the following guidelines for holding waffles for several hours or overnight or for freezing them.

➤ To keep finished waffles warm while you prepare the rest of a batch, preheat the oven to 200°F. Place each waffle, as it is made, in a single layer directly on an oven rack (not on a baking sheet). Most of the waffles in this book can be kept warm for up to 15 minutes in this manner. There are just two exceptions: The Chocolate Waffles on page 60 get too crisp when left in the oven for more than 5 minutes, and the Gingerbread Waffles on page 58 work best when baked and then left to rest and crisp at room temperature.

➤ To hold waffles up to 2 hours: Cool them on racks, then cover loosely with aluminum foil.

➤ To hold waffles several hours or overnight: Cool them on racks, then place them with cut squares of waxed or parchment paper between each in a lock-top plastic bag, and refrigerate.

➤ To hold waffles for up to two months, freeze them: Cool them on racks, then place them with cut squares of waxed or parchment paper between each in a lock-top plastic bag, and freeze.

➤ To reheat: Preheat the oven to 350°F. Lay the waffles (frozen waffles don't need to be defrosted) in a single layer directly on oven racks. Generally, waffles need about 10 minutes in the oven for reheating. However, thicker waffles might take longer, thinner ones less time. You can also reheat waffles in a toaster oven or in a toaster, but watch carefully as they can get too crisp in the latter. Don't use a microwave, which will leave the waffles soft and rubbery.

four-cup glass measure) for liquids and eggs. Depending on your recipe, you may also need a small bowl for beating egg whites.

MEASURING CUPS AND SPOONS: A set of nestled measuring cups for measuring flour and other dry ingredients, a liquid measuring cup (a four-cup size is the most practical), and a set of measuring spoons are indispensable.

RAMEKIN OR SMALL SAUCEPAN: A ramekin or small bowl is ideal for melting butter in the microwave, or you can use a small saucepan to melt butter on a cook top.

HANDHELD ELECTRIC MIXER: In waffle recipes, the dry and wet ingredients are stirred with a wooden spoon or combined with a whisk, and no beating is necessary. Many recipes, though, call for a small amount of beaten egg whites; a handheld mixer is more efficient and much easier to use than a large stand mixer for this job.

WOODEN SPOONS, WHISKS, METAL AND HEAT-PROOF RUBBER SPATULAS: A wooden spoon or whisk is ideal for combining dry and wet ingredients in waffle batters. For spreading the batter in a waffle iron, a metal spatula (especially an inexpensive offset spatula) or a heat-proof rubber spatula is useful.

COOLING RACKS: If you aren't planning to serve waffles immediately, they should be cooled on footed racks, which allow air to circulate around the waffles.

CHAPTER I

Wake Up and Smell the Waffles—

Breakfast Waffles

Nothing gets my family and houseguests out of bed faster than the aroma of fresh waffles wafting through the house. A day that starts with waffles is special, and the entries in this chapter will give you plenty of choices for the morning hour. For basic waffles that are mouthwatering good, there's Best-Ever Classic Waffles, Buttermilk Waffles, or Lighter Than Air Waffles. Multigrain Extravaganza Waffles and Whole Wheat Waffles are just as delicious, but have a more robust flavor. Serve any of these golden honeycombed cakes with cups of brewed coffee, a pitcher of freshly squeezed juice, and a side of bacon or sausage for a satisfying morning start.

Fruits and nuts make interesting additions to breakfast batters. Banana Waffles served with Maple-Pecan Syrup and Double Blueberry Waffles with berries folded into the batter will quickly become household favorites. Holiday Waffles are scented with orange and studded with pecans. The nuts add both texture and flavor to these special waffles.

Ordinary waffles can be transformed into new taste sensations with simple additions. Pumpkin purée and aromatic spices turn Pumpkin Waffles a rich golden brown. Citrus and poppy seeds give sparkle to the batter for Lemon Poppy Seed Waffles. Ginger gets a double role in Ginger Waffles with Peaches and Cream; both ground ginger and chopped crystallized ginger add zest to the batter.

For a quick and easy version of a classic breakfast food, there are simple directions for using your waffle iron to make Waffled French Toasts. You might never use a griddle again.

Any of these waffles will rescue your breakfast table from weekday boredom or provide inspiration for a leisurely weekend feast. Don't count on leftovers!

Lighter Than Air Waffles

These waffles are exceptionally light and airy (just as their name implies), due to a generous addition of cornstarch in the batter. When combined with flour, this extra ingredient produces a finer texture in waffles. These crispy golden cakes are good enough to pop right in your mouth straight from the iron or you can top them with butter and drizzle them with maple syrup or honey.

1 cup all-purpose flour
6 tablespoons cornstarch
1 tablespoon sugar
1 teaspoon baking powder
¼ teaspoon salt
¼ teaspoon baking soda
1 cup buttermilk
1 large egg, separated, plus 1 large egg white
7 tablespoons unsalted butter, melted and slightly cooled

TOPPINGS
• Butter and maple syrup
• Butter and honey

➤ Preheat a waffle iron, and if you plan to hold the waffles until serving time, preheat the oven to 200°F.

➤ In a large bowl, stir together the flour, cornstarch, sugar, baking powder, salt, and baking soda. In another bowl, whisk together the buttermilk and egg yolk until completely blended. In a small bowl, beat the egg whites until firm, but not stiff.

➤ Make a well in the dry ingredients and pour in the milk/egg mixture, blending gently only until the ingredients are combined. Add the butter in a slow stream, continuing to blend until the butter is incorporated. Gently fold in the egg whites.

➤ Pour a generous ½ cup batter (or more, depending on the size of your waffle iron) into the waffle iron and, using a metal spatula or table knife, spread batter to within ½ inch of the edge. Close the cover, and cook approximately 3 minutes, or until crisp and golden brown. Serve the waffles immediately, or place them in a single layer on racks in the preheated oven while you finish with the remaining batter.

➤ Serve the waffles with the topping of your choice.

MAKES 6 OR MORE 6½-INCH WAFFLES; SERVES 4 TO 6

Whole Wheat Waffles

These wholesome waffles are delicious topped with a generous dollop of unflavored yogurt, a sprinkling of light brown sugar, and a drizzle of honey. For special occasions, try serving them with Orange-Honey Butter or Spiced Honey Whipped Cream.

½ cup granola cereal (preferably without raisins)
¾ cup all-purpose flour
¾ cup whole wheat flour
2 teaspoons baking powder
¼ teaspoon salt
1¾ cups milk
2 large eggs, separated
2 tablespoons honey
6 tablespoons (¾ stick) unsalted butter, melted and slightly cooled

TOPPINGS
• Unflavored yogurt, light brown sugar, and honey
• Spiced Honey Whipped Cream (page 84)
• Orange-Honey Butter (page 78)

➤ Preheat a waffle iron, and if you plan to hold the waffles until serving time, preheat the oven to 200°F.

➤ Place the granola in a plastic bag and crush it with a rolling pin to break up the lumps.

➤ In a large bowl, stir together the flours, baking powder, salt, and crushed granola. In another bowl, whisk together the milk, egg yolks, and honey until completely blended. In a small bowl, beat the egg whites until firm, but not stiff.

➤ Make a well in the dry ingredients and pour in the milk/egg mixture, blending gently only until the ingredients are combined. Add the butter in a slow stream, continuing to blend until the butter is incorporated. Gently fold in the egg whites.

➤ Pour a generous ½ cup batter (or more, depending on the size of your waffle iron) into the waffle iron and, using a metal spatula or table knife, spread batter to within ½ inch of the edge. Close the cover, and cook approximately 3 minutes, or until crisp and golden brown. Serve the waffles immediately, or place them in a single layer on racks in the preheated oven while you finish with the remaining batter.

➤ Serve the waffles with the topping of your choice.

MAKES 6 OR MORE 6½-INCH WAFFLES; SERVES 4 TO 6

Buttermilk Waffles

These lightly sweetened waffles are crisp on the outside and extremely tender inside with a slightly tangy hint of buttermilk. They pair well with all manner of toppings. Night Before Blueberry Sauce and Smooth as Silk Raspberry Glaze, each accompanied respectively by fresh berries, make perfect summer partners to the waffles. Apple-Raisin Compote or Apricot-Cherry Compote are delectable cold weather garnishes.

1¾ cups all-purpose flour
4 teaspoons sugar
2 teaspoons baking powder
¼ teaspoon baking soda
¼ teaspoon salt
2 cups buttermilk
2 large eggs
6 tablespoons (¾ stick) unsalted butter, melted
   and slightly cooled

TOPPINGS
• Night Before Blueberry Sauce (page 76) and fresh
   blueberries
• Smooth as Silk Raspberry Glaze (page 76) and fresh
   raspberries
• Apple-Raisin Compote (page 88)
• Apricot-Cherry Compote (page 86)

➤ Preheat a waffle iron, and if you plan to hold the waffles until serving time, preheat the oven to 200°F.

➤ In a large bowl, stir together the flour, sugar, baking powder, baking soda, and salt. In another bowl, whisk together the buttermilk and eggs until completely blended.

➤ Make a well in the dry ingredients and pour in the milk/egg mixture, blending gently only until the ingredients are combined. Add the butter in a slow stream, continuing to blend until the butter is incorporated.

➤ Pour a generous ½ cup batter (or more, depending on the size of your waffle iron) into the waffle iron and, using a metal spatula or table knife, spread batter to within ½ inch of the edge. Close the cover, and cook approximately 3 minutes, or until crisp and golden brown. Serve the waffles immediately, or place them in a single layer on racks in the preheated oven while you finish with the remaining batter.

➤ Serve the waffles with the topping of your choice.

MAKES 6 OR MORE 6½-INCH WAFFLES; SERVES 4 TO 6

Multigrain Extravaganza Waffles

The flours and seeds called for in these waffles can be found at natural foods stores and in some supermarkets. High in fiber and rich in nutrients, these "good for you" waffles could easily become your favorite, with their hearty taste and crunchy texture. Serve them with maple syrup and butter or with sliced strawberries and bananas topped with yogurt and drizzled with honey.

1 cup whole wheat flour
½ cup spelt flour
½ cup oat bran flour (see Note)
¼ cup roasted, unsalted sunflower seeds
¼ cup rolled oats (not quick oats)
3 tablespoons packed light brown sugar
2 tablespoons flax seeds
2 tablespoons millet seeds
2½ teaspoons baking powder
½ teaspoon salt
1½ cups milk
2 large eggs
8 tablespoons (1 stick) unsalted butter, melted and slightly cooled

TOPPINGS
- Maple syrup and butter
- Sliced strawberries and bananas, unflavored yogurt, and honey

➤ Preheat a waffle iron, and if you plan to hold the waffles until serving time, preheat the oven to 200°F.

➤ In a large bowl, stir together the flours, sunflower seeds, oats, brown sugar, flax and millet seeds, baking powder, and salt. In a medium bowl, whisk together the milk and eggs until completely blended.

➤ Make a well in the dry ingredients and pour in the milk/egg mixture, blending gently only until the ingredients are combined. Add the butter in a slow stream, continuing to blend until the butter is incorporated.

➤ Pour a generous ½ cup batter (or more, depending on the size of your waffle iron) into the waffle iron and, using a metal spatula or table knife, spread batter to within ½ inch of the edge. Close the cover, and cook approximately 3 minutes, or until crisp and golden brown. Serve the waffles immediately, or place them in a single layer on racks in the preheated oven while you finish with the remaining batter.

➤ Serve the waffles with the topping of your choice.

MAKES 6 OR MORE 6½-INCH WAFFLES; SERVES 4 TO 6

NOTE: If you can't find oat bran flour, you can substitute oat bran cereal.

Lemon Poppy Seed Waffles

Lemon yogurt, as well as lemon juice and zest, lend a light and delicate lemon flavor to these waffles. Poppy seeds, a traditional partner to this citrus fruit, add texture and bits of color. When served with mounds of Lemon Chantilly Cream and fresh blueberries, they make a fabulous offering for a special breakfast or brunch.

2 cups all-purpose flour
¼ cup sugar
2 tablespoons poppy seeds
2 teaspoons baking powder
½ teaspoon baking soda
¼ teaspoon salt
Two 6-ounce containers lemon yogurt (see Note)
¾ cup milk
6 tablespoons freshly squeezed lemon juice
2 large eggs, separated
6 tablespoons (¾ stick) unsalted butter, melted and
    slightly cooled
2 tablespoons grated lemon zest

TOPPING
• Confectioners' sugar; Lemon Chantilly Cream
   (page 83); 2 cups fresh blueberries, strawberries,
   raspberries, or any combination

➤ Preheat a waffle iron, and if you plan to hold the waffles until serving time, preheat the oven to 200°F.

➤ In a large bowl, stir together the flour, sugar, poppy seeds, baking powder, baking soda, and salt. In another bowl, whisk together the yogurt, milk, lemon juice, and egg yolks until completely blended. In a small bowl, beat the egg whites until firm, but not stiff.

➤ Make a well in the dry ingredients and pour in the milk/egg mixture, blending gently only until the ingredients are combined. Add the butter in a slow stream, continuing to blend until the butter is incorporated. Gently fold in the egg whites, then sprinkle the lemon zest over the batter and fold it in.

➤ Pour a generous ½ cup batter (or more, depending on the size of your waffle iron) into the waffle iron and, using a metal spatula or table knife, spread batter to within ½ inch of the edge. Close the cover, and cook approximately 3 minutes, or until crisp and golden brown. Serve the waffles immediately, or place them in a single layer on racks in the preheated oven while you finish with the remaining batter.

➤ Serve the waffles with a dusting of confectioners' sugar, a bowl of Lemon Chantilly Cream, and a bowl of berries.

MAKES 6 OR MORE 6½-INCH WAFFLES; SERVES 4 TO 6

NOTE: Lemon yogurts vary in the intensity of their citrus flavor depending on the brand and whether they are regular or reduced fat. Often, the reduced and nonfat varieties have a stronger lemon flavor than the whole fat ones. Any will work in this recipe.

Banana Waffles

liced bananas and a hint of cinnamon turn an ordinary waffle batter into something extra special in the following recipe. These waffles, which can be eaten piping hot straight off the iron unadorned, are even more irresistible when drizzled with warm Maple-Pecan Syrup or topped with Pecan Toffee Crunch Butter.

1¾ cups all-purpose flour
3 tablespoons packed light brown sugar
1 tablespoon baking powder
½ teaspoon salt
¼ teaspoon ground cinnamon
¼ teaspoon baking soda
1¼ cups milk
½ cup sour cream
2 large eggs, separated
½ teaspoon vanilla extract
4 ripe medium bananas
8 tablespoons (1 stick) unsalted butter, melted and
   slightly cooled

TOPPINGS
• Maple-Pecan Syrup (page 82)
• Pecan Toffee Crunch Butter (page 79)

➤ Preheat a waffle iron, and if you plan to hold the waffles until serving time, preheat the oven to 200°F.

➤ In a large bowl, stir together the flour, brown sugar, baking powder, salt, cinnamon, and baking soda. In another bowl, whisk together the milk, sour cream, egg yolks, and vanilla until completely blended. Slice the bananas, crosswise, into thin rounds and toss them in a medium bowl with the butter. In a small bowl, beat the egg whites until firm, but not stiff.

➤ Make a well in the dry ingredients and pour in the milk/egg mixture, blending gently only until the ingredients are combined. Fold in the bananas and butter. Then gently fold in the egg whites.

➤ Pour a generous ½ cup batter (or more, depending on the size of your waffle iron) into the waffle iron and, using a metal spatula or table knife, spread batter to within ½ inch of the edge. Close the cover, and cook approximately 3 minutes, or until slightly crisp and golden brown. Serve the waffles immediately, or place them in a single layer on racks in the preheated oven while you finish with the remaining batter.

➤ Serve the waffles with the topping of your choice.

MAKES 6 OR MORE 6½-INCH WAFFLES; SERVES 4 TO 6

Double Blueberry Waffles

Blueberries play a dual role in these waffles. They are folded into the batter so that when you bite into one of the cooked, blue-speckled waffles, you get a juicy taste of the berries. Blueberries are also used in the luscious spiced blueberry sauce that is drizzled over the piping hot waffles.

1½ cups all-purpose flour
4 teaspoons baking powder
2 teaspoons sugar
1 teaspoon ground cinnamon
½ teaspoon salt
1¾ cups milk
2 large eggs, separated
1 teaspoon grated lemon zest
8 tablespoons (1 stick) unsalted butter, melted and
    slightly cooled
1½ cups blueberries

TOPPING
• Night Before Blueberry Sauce (page 76)

➤ Preheat a waffle iron, and if you plan to hold the waffles until serving time, preheat the oven to 200°F.

➤ In a large bowl, stir together the flour, baking powder, sugar, cinnamon, and salt. In another bowl, whisk together the milk, egg yolks, and lemon zest until completely blended. In a small bowl, beat the egg whites until firm, but not stiff.

➤ Make a well in the dry ingredients and pour in the milk/egg mixture, blending gently only until the ingredients are combined. Add the butter in a slow stream, continuing to blend until the butter is incorporated. Gently fold in the egg whites and blueberries.

➤ Pour a generous ½ cup batter (or more, depending on the size of your waffle iron) into the waffle iron and, using a metal spatula or table knife, spread batter to within ½ inch of the edge. Close the cover, and cook approximately 3 minutes, or until crisp and golden brown. Serve the waffles immediately, or place them in a single layer on racks in the preheated oven while you finish with the remaining batter.

➤ Serve the waffles with Night Before Blueberry Sauce.

MAKES 6 OR MORE 6½-INCH WAFFLES; SERVES 4 TO 6

Pumpkin Waffles

Although I love to serve these hearty waffles, flavored with pumpkin purée and aromatic spices, in the fall when the days turn cool and crisp, the truth is they make breakfast or brunch special any time of the year. You can make them more festive with crunchy Pecan Toffee Crunch Butter or Whipped Maple Cream and a sprinkle of nuts.

1¼ cups all-purpose flour
3 tablespoons packed light brown sugar
2 teaspoons baking powder
½ teaspoon ground cinnamon
¼ teaspoon salt
⅛ teaspoon ground ginger
Pinch ground cloves
Pinch ground nutmeg
1 cup milk
¾ cup cooked pumpkin purée (Use plain pumpkin purée, not pumpkin pie filling.)
2 large eggs, separated
4 tablespoons (½ stick) unsalted butter, melted and slightly cooled

TOPPINGS
• Maple syrup and butter
• Pecan Toffee Crunch Butter (page 79)
• Whipped Maple Cream (page 84) plus ½ cup chopped toasted pecans or walnuts (see Note)

➤ Preheat a waffle iron, and if you plan to hold the waffles until serving time, preheat the oven to 200°F.

➤ In a large bowl, stir together the flour, brown sugar, baking powder, cinnamon, salt, ginger, cloves, and nutmeg. In another bowl, whisk together the milk, pumpkin purée, and egg yolks until completely blended. In a small bowl, beat the egg whites until firm, but not stiff.

➤ Make a well in the dry ingredients and pour in the milk/egg mixture, blending gently only until the ingredients are combined. Add the butter in a slow stream, continuing to blend until the butter is incorporated. Gently fold in the egg whites.

➤ Pour a generous ½ cup batter (or more, depending on the size of your waffle iron) into the waffle iron and, using a metal spatula or table knife, spread batter to within ½ inch of the edge. Close the cover, and cook approximately 3 minutes, or until crisp and golden brown. Serve the waffles immediately, or place them in a single layer on racks in the preheated oven while you finish with the remaining batter.

➤ Serve the waffles with the topping of your choice.

MAKES 6 OR MORE 6½-INCH WAFFLES; SERVES 4 TO 6

NOTE: To toast pecans, walnuts, or almonds: Arrange an oven rack at center position and preheat the oven to 350°F. Spread the nuts on a baking sheet with sides and bake until lightly browned. Almonds will take about 8 minutes, pecans 5 to 6 minutes, and walnuts 5 to 8 minutes. Watch carefully so the nuts do not burn. Remove them from the oven and cool.

Ginger Waffles with Peaches and Cream

Small bits of crystallized ginger impart sweet and piquant accents to this batter, while ground ginger provides a spicy undertone. These waffles make a glorious sight topped with sliced fresh peaches and mounds of whipped cream. Or, drizzle the peaches with some Smooth as Silk Raspberry Glaze (page 76) before topping them with whipped cream.

1¾ cups all-purpose flour
2½ tablespoons very finely chopped crystallized ginger
1 tablespoon sugar
1 tablespoon ground ginger
1 teaspoon baking powder
½ teaspoon baking soda
¼ teaspoon salt
1½ cups buttermilk
2 large eggs, separated
1 teaspoon vanilla extract
4 tablespoons (½ stick) unsalted butter, melted and slightly cooled

PEACHES AND CREAM TOPPING
2 cups (4 to 5 peaches) peeled, thinly sliced yellow peaches
2 teaspoons freshly squeezed lemon juice
1 to 2 teaspoons sugar
1 cup heavy (whipping) cream
4 teaspoons confectioners' sugar, plus extra (for dusting)

➤ Preheat a waffle iron, and if you plan to hold the waffles until serving time, preheat the oven to 200°F.

➤ In a large bowl, stir together the flour, crystallized ginger, sugar, ground ginger, baking powder, baking soda, and salt. In another bowl, whisk together the buttermilk, egg yolks, and vanilla until completely blended. In a small bowl, beat the egg whites until firm, but not stiff.

➤ Make a well in the dry ingredients and pour in the milk/egg mixture, blending gently only until the ingredients are combined. Add the butter in a slow stream, continuing to blend until the butter is incorporated. Gently fold in the egg whites.

➤ Pour a generous ½ cup batter (or more, depending on the size of your waffle iron) into the waffle iron and, using a metal spatula or table knife, spread batter to within ½ inch of the edge. Close the cover, and cook approximately 3 minutes, or until crisp and golden brown. Serve the waffles immediately, or place them in a single layer on racks in the preheated oven while you finish with the remaining batter.

➤ To prepare the peaches and cream topping: Toss the peaches in a bowl with the lemon juice and 1 teaspoon sugar. Taste and, if desired, toss with additional sugar. Whip the cream until soft peaks form, then add the confectioners' sugar and beat until just firm.

➤ Place a waffle on each of 6 plates and top each with peaches and a dollop of whipped cream. Dust them generously with confectioners' sugar.

MAKES 6 OR MORE 6½-INCH WAFFLES; SERVES 4 TO 6

Holiday Waffles

hen cranberries and pecans are added to a delicious orange-scented batter, the result is a festive waffle perfect to use for holiday entertaining. These crispy fruit- and nut-studded waffles, dusted with confectioners' sugar and napped with warm, crimson-hued Cranberry Syrup, make tempting fare during the season of celebrations.

1½ cups all-purpose flour
1 cup dried cranberries
½ cup chopped pecans
4 teaspoons sugar
1 tablespoon baking powder
¼ teaspoon baking soda
¼ teaspoon salt
1 cup milk
1 cup freshly squeezed orange juice
2 large eggs, separated
1 tablespoon grated orange zest
6 tablespoons (¾ stick) unsalted butter, melted and
  slightly cooled

TOPPING
• Confectioners' sugar (for dusting) and Cranberry
  Syrup (page 80), warmed

➤ Preheat a waffle iron, and if you plan to hold the waffles until serving time, preheat the oven to 200°F.

➤ In a large bowl, stir together the flour, cranberries, pecans, sugar, baking powder, baking soda, and salt. In a medium bowl, whisk together the milk, orange juice, and egg yolks until completely blended. In a small bowl, beat the egg whites until firm, but not stiff.

➤ Make a well in the dry ingredients and pour in the milk/egg mixture, blending gently only until the ingredients are combined. Stir the orange zest into the butter, then add the butter in a slow stream, continuing to blend until the butter is incorporated. Gently fold in the egg whites.

➤ Pour a generous ½ cup batter (or more, depending on the size of your waffle iron) into the waffle iron and, using a metal spatula or table knife, spread batter to within ½ inch of the edge. Close the cover, and cook approximately 3 minutes, or until crisp and golden brown. Serve the waffles immediately, or place them in a single layer on racks in the preheated oven while you finish with the remaining batter.

➤ To serve, dust the waffles with confectioners' sugar and drizzle with warm Cranberry Syrup.

MAKES 6 OR MORE 6½-INCH WAFFLES; SERVES 4 TO 6

Best-Ever Classic Waffles

sing a smaller than usual quantity of flour and a generous amount of butter makes these golden waffles exceptionally crisp and tender. They are delicious served simply with a pitcher of maple syrup and pats of butter, and equally tempting offered with Night Before Blueberry Sauce or Summertime Strawberry Sauce.

1½ cups all-purpose flour
4 teaspoons baking powder
2 teaspoons sugar
½ teaspoon salt
1¾ cups milk
2 large eggs, separated
8 tablespoons (1 stick) unsalted butter, melted and
  slightly cooled

TOPPINGS
• Maple syrup and butter
• Night Before Blueberry Sauce (page 76)
• Summertime Strawberry Sauce (page 75)

➤ Preheat a waffle iron, and if you plan to hold the waffles until serving time, preheat the oven to 200°F.

➤ In a large bowl, stir together the flour, baking powder, sugar, and salt. In another bowl, whisk together the milk and egg yolks until completely blended. In a small bowl, beat the egg whites until firm, but not stiff.

➤ Make a well in the dry ingredients and pour in the milk/egg mixture, blending gently only until the ingredients are combined. Add the butter in a slow stream, continuing to blend until the butter is incorporated. Gently fold in the egg whites.

➤ Pour a generous ½ cup batter (or more, depending on the size of your waffle iron) into the waffle iron and, using a metal spatula or table knife, spread batter to within ½ inch of the edge. Close the cover, and cook approximately 3 minutes, or until crisp and golden brown. Serve the waffles immediately, or place them in a single layer on racks in the preheated oven while you finish with the remaining batter.

➤ Serve the waffles with the topping of your choice.

MAKES 6 OR MORE 6½-INCH WAFFLES; SERVES 4 TO 6

Waffled French Toasts

I learned from my colleague, Dorie Greenspan, that a waffle iron could be used to toast bread. Then, it didn't take me long to discover that French toast could be prepared in a waffle iron too. You simply pop egg-and-milk-soaked bread slices into a waffle iron, and, a few minutes later, remove golden crisp "waffled" toasts. Although you can experiment with different breads, I've found that thick white or challah slices work best. Serve the toasts with maple syrup and butter or offer them with a warm compote topping or Night Before Blueberry Sauce.

4 large eggs
½ cup half-and-half
2 tablespoons sugar
½ teaspoon vanilla extract
¼ teaspoon ground cinnamon
Twelve ½-inch-thick slices good-quality white or egg bread (see Note)

TOPPINGS
• Maple syrup and butter
• Cranberry-Apple Compote (page 89)
• Apricot-Cherry Compote (page 86)
• Night Before Blueberry Sauce (page 76)
  Confectioners' sugar (for dusting)

➤ Preheat a waffle iron, and preheat the oven to 200°F.

➤ In a shallow bowl, whisk together the eggs, half-and-half, sugar, vanilla, and cinnamon until completely blended. Add a bread slice to the mixture and turn several times until it is saturated with liquid. Then lift it up and let excess liquid fall back into the bowl. Transfer the bread to the waffle iron. (If your waffle iron can accommodate 2 slices at a time, repeat with an additional slice of bread.) Close the cover, and cook approximately 3 minutes, or until golden brown. Place the toasts in a single layer on racks in the preheated oven while you continue with the remaining bread.

➤ Arrange 2 toasts on each of 6 dinner plates. Dust with confectioners' sugar and serve with the topping of your choice

SERVES 6

 NOTE: Pepperidge Farm Toasting White, Thomas' Original Toasting Bread, or a good challah (egg bread) work well in this recipe. Peasant and country breads, which have denser textures, do not absorb the egg mixture as well.

CHAPTER II

Waffles All Day—

Savory Waffles

Long thought of as breakfast fare, waffles have found their way to the dinner table. As early as the 1930s, creative American cooks — perhaps prodded by the Great Depression — began serving them for lunch and supper. Waffles capped with creamed chicken or with cheese and tomatoes became favorites for such meals. Today's marketplace provides endless opportunities to create savory waffles for brunch, lunch, supper, or even a late night snack. The following pages feature a cornucopia of ingredients and seasonings that move waffles from early morning to midday or evening fare.

Cornbread Waffles napped with a velvety smooth sauce of creamed chicken and fennel are redolent of those early twentieth century waffles. Another old-fashioned creation is made with sausages and apples that are sautéed in a mustard and apple jelly glaze, then mounded atop crisp waffles.

Curry powder, currants, and walnuts, for example, enhance a savory batter in Indian Spiced Waffles. The yellow-hued waffles are delicious paired with warm Plum Chutney. Equally tempting are Sour Cream Waffles with fresh dill that are served with smoked salmon, chopped red onion, and lemon.

Grated pepper Jack cheese and ground cumin add assertive accents to Southwest cornmeal waffles served with an avocado salsa. Corn kernels and a dash of Tabasco give zest to buttermilk waffles topped with a piquant tomato and pepper salsa.

Eggs Benedict from New Orleans and croque-monsieur sandwiches from France get reinterpreted as savory waffle entrées. Waffles replace English muffins in the former and are used instead of toasted bread in the latter. Both yield tantalizing results.

Such savory inventions will, I hope, whet your appetite and encourage you to serve waffles any time of the day — from morning to midnight!

Herbed Waffles Topped with Asparagus and Creamy Boursin Sauce

A trio of fresh herbs—parsley, chives, and rosemary—enhances the savory waffle batter in this recipe. Baked until golden and crisp, the waffles are delicious topped with blanched asparagus spears and a creamy sauce made with Boursin cheese and half-and-half. Offer a spinach and red leaf salad tossed in a red wine vinaigrette as an accompaniment.

ASPARAGUS AND CREAMY BOURSIN SAUCE
One 5.2-ounce package Boursin Cheese with Herbs
1 cup half-and-half
1½ pounds thin asparagus, tough ends trimmed
1 tablespoon salt, plus more for seasoning
2 tablespoons unsalted butter

HERBED WAFFLES
1½ cups all-purpose flour
4 teaspoons baking powder
½ teaspoon salt
1¾ cups milk
2 large eggs, separated
4 tablespoons (½ stick) unsalted butter, melted and slightly cooled
2 tablespoons plus ½ teaspoon chopped fresh Italian parsley, divided
2 tablespoons plus ½ teaspoon chopped fresh chives, divided
1 tablespoon plus ½ teaspoon chopped fresh rosemary, divided

➤ To make the Asparagus and Creamy Boursin Sauce: Break the cheese into small chunks and put them in a medium saucepan along with the half-and-half. Place over medium heat and whisk until the cheese melts and the mixture is smooth and warm. Cover and set aside.

➤ Fill a large saucepan ⅔ full with water and bring it to a boil. Add the asparagus and salt. Cook until tender when pierced with a knife, 3 to 4 minutes. Drain in a colander, refresh under cold running water to keep bright green, and set aside.

➤ To make the Herbed Waffles: Preheat a waffle iron, and if you plan to hold the waffles until serving time, preheat the oven to 200°F.

➤ In a medium bowl, stir together the flour, baking powder, and salt. In another bowl, whisk together the milk and egg yolks until completely blended. In a small bowl, beat the egg whites until firm, but not stiff.

➤ Make a well in the dry ingredients and pour in the milk/egg mixture, blending gently only until the ingredients are combined. Add the butter in a slow stream, continuing to blend until the butter is incorporated. Stir in 2 tablespoons of the parsley, 2 tablespoons of the chives, and 1 tablespoon of the rosemary. Gently fold in the egg whites.

Continued

➤ Pour a generous ½ cup batter (or more, depending on the size of your waffle iron) into the waffle iron and, using a metal spatula or table knife, spread batter to within ½ inch of the edge. Close the cover, and cook approximately 3 minutes, or until crisp and golden brown. Serve the waffles immediately, or place them in a single layer on racks in the preheated oven while you finish with the remaining batter.

➤ While the waffles are in the oven, melt the 2 tablespoons butter in a large, heavy skillet over medium-high heat until hot. Add the asparagus and toss and cook until hot. Season with salt.

➤ To serve, arrange a waffle on each of 6 dinner plates. (Save extra waffles for another use.) Garnish each serving with a small bundle of asparagus and spoon some Creamy Boursin Sauce over it. Mix together the remaining herbs and sprinkle them over the waffles.

SERVES 6

Sour Cream Waffles with Smoked Salmon

These waffles, made with both white and whole wheat flours, were modeled after Russian pancakes, called blini. Thin slices of smoked salmon, rolled into cornucopias, perch atop the baked waffles. Chopped red onion, fresh dill, lemon, and sour cream add to the waffles' glory. Serve these waffles at a special brunch along with a cucumber salad.

SMOKED SALMON, DILL, AND RED ONION TOPPING
12 ounces sliced smoked salmon
¾ cup sour cream
2 tablespoons freshly squeezed lemon juice
¾ cup chopped red onion
3 tablespoons chopped fresh dill
1 tablespoon grated lemon zest (2 to 3 lemons)

SOUR CREAM WAFFLES
1¼ cups all-purpose flour
½ cup whole wheat flour
1 teaspoon freshly ground black pepper
½ teaspoon salt
1 cup plus 2 tablespoons milk
2 large eggs, separated
3 tablespoons sour cream
3 tablespoons unsalted butter, melted and slightly cooled
¼ cup chopped fresh dill

➤ Have all the ingredients for the topping measured and ready. Roll the salmon slices into cornucopia or cone shapes. Set aside.

➤ To make the Sour Cream Waffles: Preheat a waffle iron, and if you plan to hold the waffles until serving time, preheat the oven to 200°F.

➤ In a large bowl, stir together the flours, pepper, and salt. In another bowl, whisk together the milk, egg yolks, and sour cream until completely blended. In a small bowl, beat the egg whites until firm, but not stiff.

➤ Make a well in the dry ingredients and pour in the milk/egg mixture, blending gently only until the ingredients are combined. Add the butter in a slow stream, continuing to blend until the butter is incorporated. Gently fold in the egg whites and then the dill.

➤ Pour a generous ½ cup batter (or more, depending on the size of your waffle iron) into the waffle iron and, using a metal spatula or table knife, spread batter to within ½ inch of the edge. Close the cover, and cook approximately 3 minutes, or until crisp and golden brown. Serve the waffles immediately, or place them in a single layer on racks in the preheated oven while you finish with the remaining batter.

➤ To serve, arrange a waffle on each of 6 dinner plates. (Save extra waffles for another use.) Garnish the center of each waffle with 2 tablespoons of sour cream. Arrange 3 to 4 rolled salmon slices in a spoke pattern on top of each waffle. Drizzle the salmon with some lemon juice. Sprinkle each waffle with the red onions, dill, and lemon zest.

SERVES 6

Crisp Waffles with Mustard-Glazed Sausages and Apples

A piquant mixture of heated apple jelly and mustard makes a perfect glaze for sautéed sausage links and apples. This hearty topping is delicious served atop such crispy waffles as Multigrain Extravaganza Waffles or Corn Waffles. This is comfort food at its best for brunch or supper on a chilly day.

1 recipe Multigrain Extravaganza Waffles (page 23) or
Corn Waffles with Tomato and Yellow Pepper Salsa
(page 49)

SAUSAGE AND APPLE TOPPING
1 cup apple jelly
¾ cup sweet-hot mustard (see Note)
3 Golden Delicious apples
4 tablespoons (½ stick) unsalted butter
1 pound flavorful, mild, breakfast sausage links (see Note)
1 tablespoon chopped fresh sage plus 6 fresh sage sprigs

➤ Prepare the waffles according to directions and keep warm in a single layer on racks in a 200°F oven.

➤ To make the Sausage and Apple Topping: Put the jelly and mustard in a medium, heavy, nonreactive saucepan set over medium heat. Whisk constantly until liquefied and hot, about 3 minutes or more. Remove from the heat.

➤ Core, stem, and halve the unpeeled apples. Cut each half into ½-inch wedges.

➤ Melt the butter in a large, heavy skillet over medium-high heat. When hot, add the sausages and cook, turning several times, until browned on all sides and cooked through, 5 minutes or more. Add the apples and cook, stirring, until the apples are just tender, about 2 minutes more. (Do not overcook or the apples will become mushy.) Pour the jelly/mustard sauce into the skillet, and stir and cook 1 minute more. Remove from the heat and cover loosely with aluminum foil while you prepare the waffles.

➤ To serve, arrange a waffle on each of 6 dinner plates. (Save extra waffles for another use.) Using a slotted spoon, mound some sausages and apples over each waffle. Then spoon some of the remaining sauce in the skillet over each serving. Sprinkle each serving with the chopped sage and garnish with a sage sprig.

SERVES 6

 NOTE: Sweet Hot Mister Mustard works well in this recipe and is available in most groceries. Both traditional pork breakfast sausages and turkey breakfast sausages work well with the glaze. The important thing is to use sausages that are well seasoned but mild.

Waffles Benedict

or a new twist on an old tradition, waffles replace English muffins in this version of eggs Benedict.

HOLLANDAISE SAUCE
12 tablespoons (1½ sticks) unsalted butter, diced
3 large egg yolks
1½ tablespoons light cream
½ teaspoon kosher salt
Generous pinch cayenne pepper
1 tablespoon freshly squeezed lemon juice

1 recipe Best-Ever Classic Waffles (page 33), prepared without sugar

POACHED EGGS AND PROSCIUTTO TOPPING
6 large eggs
6 ounces thinly sliced prosciutto
Kosher salt
Freshly ground black pepper
2 tablespoons chopped fresh Italian parsley

➤ Preheat the oven to 200°F.

➤ To make the Hollandaise Sauce (see Note): Have ready a deep-sided skillet filled halfway with barely simmering water. Melt the butter in a medium, heavy saucepan set over medium heat until quite hot, but not brown. Remove. Put the egg yolks, cream, salt, and cayenne in a blender or in the bowl of a food processor fitted with the metal blade. Blend or process until the mixture is smooth. With the machine running, add the butter gradually, in a thin stream. As the butter is added, the sauce will thicken. Add the lemon juice and process

a few seconds more. Transfer the sauce to a medium heat-proof bowl and place the bowl in the pan of barely simmering water to keep warm for up to 1 hour.

➤ Prepare the waffles according to directions and keep warm in a single layer on racks in the preheated oven while you poach the eggs.

➤ To make the Poached Eggs and Prosciutto Topping: If you have an egg poacher, follow the manufacturer's directions and poach the eggs until the whites are set but the yolks are still runny. Otherwise, fill a large skillet two-thirds full of water and set it over medium heat until the water is simmering. Reduce the heat, and break the eggs gently into the water. Cook until the whites are set but the yolks are still runny, 3 to 4 minutes.

➤ While the eggs are poaching, arrange a waffle on each of 6 dinner plates and top each with several slices of the prosciutto. (Save extra waffles for another use.) Remove the eggs with a slotted spoon, placing 1 in the center of each waffle. Salt and pepper the eggs, then spoon some of the hollandaise over each. Sprinkle with the parsley. Serve immediately.

SERVES 6

NOTE: Hand method for making the hollandaise: Melt the butter in a medium saucepan over medium heat. Whisk together the egg yolks, cream, lemon juice, salt, and cayenne in the top of a double boiler set over but not touching simmering water. Gradually whisk in the butter. Continue to cook, whisking constantly, until the sauce thickens and coats the back of a spoon. The sauce can be prepared in advance and kept warm as in the blender/processor method.

Indian Spiced Waffles with Plum Chutney

Indian food, with its vibrant flavors, has long been a favorite of mine, so I decided to try using some robust seasonings redolent of this cuisine in a savory waffle creation. A generous amount of curry powder, as well as chopped walnuts and currants added to the batter, yields crisp golden waffles that are irresistible when topped with Plum Chutney.

TOPPING
• Plum Chutney (page 92)

INDIAN SPICED WAFFLES
1½ cups all-purpose flour
4 teaspoons baking powder
2 teaspoons curry powder
½ teaspoon salt
1¾ cups milk
2 large eggs, separated
8 tablespoons (1 stick) unsalted butter, melted and
   slightly cooled
½ cup chopped walnuts
½ cup dried currants

➤ Prepare the Plum Chutney according to the directions. Set it aside and reheat when needed, if necessary.

➤ To make the Indian Spiced Waffles: Preheat a waffle iron, and if you plan to hold the waffles until serving time, preheat the oven to 200°F.

➤ In a large bowl, stir together the flour, baking powder, curry powder, and salt. In another bowl, whisk together the milk and egg yolks until completely blended. In a small bowl, beat the egg whites until firm, but not stiff.

➤ Make a well in the dry ingredients and pour in the milk/egg mixture, blending gently only until the ingredients are combined. Add the butter in a slow stream, continuing to blend until the butter is incorporated. Fold in the walnuts and currants and then gently fold in the egg whites.

➤ Pour a generous ½ cup batter (or more, depending on the size of your waffle iron) into the waffle iron and, using a metal spatula or table knife, spread batter to within ½ inch of the edge. Close the cover, and cook approximately 3 minutes, or until crisp and golden brown. Serve the waffles immediately, or place them in a single layer on racks in the preheated oven while you finish with the remaining batter.

➤ To serve, arrange a waffle on each of 6 dinner plates. (Save extra waffles for another use.) Serve the waffles with the Plum Chutney.

SERVES 6

Cornbread Waffles with Creamed Chicken and Fennel

These hearty country-style waffles, with their dense cornmeal texture, pair perfectly with a savory creamed chicken and vegetable topping. The sauce can be completely prepared a day in advance. Rich and satisfying, this all-in-one main course makes a comforting meal on a chilly day. For a variation, try topping these waffles with your favorite rich, thick chili.

CREAMED CHICKEN AND FENNEL TOPPING
2 large fennel bulbs
4 cups reduced-sodium chicken broth
1½ cups (about 8 ounces) sliced baby carrots
1 cup fresh or frozen peas
2 cups diced cooked chicken, preferably white meat (see Note)
3 ounces thinly sliced prosciutto, cut into 2-by-¼-inch strips
4 tablespoons (½ stick) unsalted butter
¼ cup all-purpose flour
1½ cups light cream
2 tablespoons freshly squeezed lemon juice
2 teaspoons fennel seeds, crushed
1 teaspoon kosher salt
¼ cup chopped fresh Italian parsley

CORNBREAD WAFFLES
1 cup yellow cornmeal (Use regular, not coarsely ground, cornmeal.)
1 cup all-purpose flour
1 teaspoon baking powder
½ teaspoon baking soda
½ teaspoon salt
¼ teaspoon cayenne pepper
1⅓ cups buttermilk
2 large eggs
6 tablespoons (¾ stick) unsalted butter, melted and slightly cooled

➤ To make the Creamed Chicken and Fennel Topping: Trim and discard the lacy stalks from the fennel. Halve the bulbs lengthwise; cut out and discard the tough cores. Chop enough fennel to yield 1½ cups.

➤ Bring the broth to a simmer in a medium saucepan over medium-high heat. Add the fennel and carrots and cook until the vegetables are tender when pierced with a knife, about 12 minutes. Add the peas after 10 minutes. Strain the vegetables and reserve 1½ cups of the broth.

➤ Mix the vegetables, chicken, and prosciutto in a large bowl and set aside.

➤ Melt the butter in a large, heavy saucepan over medium-high heat. Add the flour and cook, stirring, 1 minute or less. Gradually whisk in the cream and reserved broth. Whisk until the mixture thickens slightly and coats the back of a spoon, 4 minutes or longer. Stir in the lemon juice, fennel seeds, and salt. Stir in the chicken, prosciutto, and vegetables and season with more salt if needed. (If preparing the creamed chicken ahead, refrigerate the sauce and the chicken/vegetable mixture separately. Reheat, combining the two in a large saucepan set over medium heat, stirring constantly.)

➤ To make the Cornbread Waffles: Preheat a waffle iron, and if you plan to hold the waffles until serving time, preheat the oven to 200°F.

➤ In a large bowl, stir together the cornmeal, flour, baking powder, baking soda, salt, and cayenne. In a medium bowl, whisk together the buttermilk and eggs until completely blended.

➤ Make a well in the dry ingredients and pour in the milk/egg mixture, blending gently only until the ingredients are combined. Add the butter in a slow stream, continuing to blend until the butter is incorporated. The batter will be very thick.

➤ Pour a generous ½ cup batter (or more, depending on the size of your waffle iron) into the waffle iron and, using a metal spatula or table knife, spread batter to within ½ inch of the edge. Close the cover, and cook approximately 3 minutes, or until crisp and golden brown. Serve the waffles immediately, or place them in a single layer on racks in the preheated oven while you finish with the remaining batter.

➤ To serve, arrange a waffle on each of 6 dinner plates. (Save extra waffles for another use.) Spoon some creamed chicken mixture over each and sprinkle with the parsley.

SERVES 6

 NOTE: You can use your own leftover roast chicken in this recipe or buy a plain unseasoned roast chicken from the grocery.

Corn Waffles with Tomato and Yellow Pepper Salsa

Bright golden sautéed corn kernels fleck these buttermilk waffles that are prepared with both white flour and yellow cornmeal. A hint of Tabasco sauce adds subtle heat. Topped with a fresh salsa made with tomatoes and yellow bell peppers, these savory waffles become a tempting all-in-one entrée to serve family and friends for brunch, lunch, or a light supper.

TOPPING
• Tomato and Yellow Pepper Salsa (page 91)

CORN WAFFLES
4½ tablespoons unsalted butter, melted, divided
1¼ cups fresh corn kernels (scraped from 3 large ears) or thawed frozen corn, patted dry
1 cup all-purpose flour
½ cup yellow cornmeal (Use regular, not coarsely ground, cornmeal.)
½ cup grated sharp white Cheddar cheese
1½ teaspoons baking powder
½ teaspoon salt
⅜ teaspoon baking soda
1½ cups buttermilk
1 large egg, separated, plus 1 large egg yolk
¾ teaspoon Tabasco sauce

➤ Prepare the Tomato and Yellow Pepper Salsa according to the directions and set aside.

➤ To make the Corn Waffles: Preheat a waffle iron, and if you plan to hold the waffles until serving time, preheat the oven to 200°F.

➤ Put 1½ tablespoons of the butter in a large skillet over medium-high heat. When hot, add the corn and cook, stirring, until light golden brown, 2 to 3 minutes, and then set aside. (If using frozen kernels, cook an extra 2 to 3 minutes.)

➤ In a large bowl, stir together the flour, cornmeal, cheese, baking powder, salt, and baking soda. In another bowl, whisk together the buttermilk, egg yolks, and Tabasco until completely blended. In a small bowl, beat the egg white until firm, but not stiff.

➤ Make a well in the dry ingredients and pour in the milk/egg mixture, blending gently only until the ingredients are combined. Add the remaining 3 tablespoons butter in a slow stream, continuing to blend until the butter is incorporated. Gently fold in the egg white and corn.

➤ Pour a generous ½ cup batter (or more, depending on the size of your waffle iron) into the waffle iron and, using a metal spatula or table knife, spread batter to within ½ inch of the edge. Close the cover, and cook approximately 3 minutes, or until crisp and golden brown. Serve the waffles immediately, or place them in a single layer on racks in the preheated oven while you finish with the remaining batter.

➤ To serve, arrange a waffle on each of 6 dinner plates. (Save extra waffles for another use.) Serve the waffles with a generous dollop of Tomato and Yellow Pepper Salsa.

SERVES 6

Croque-Monsieur Waffles

France's celebrated grilled cheese and ham sandwich, the croque-monsieur, gets reinvented in this recipe, in which crisp waffles replace bread. The waffles are topped with thin slices of Gruyère cheese and ham, spread with a white sauce, then sprinkled with grated Gruyère. Popped under the broiler until the cheese melts, these waffles make a special dish to serve for brunch, lunch, or a light supper. A green salad tossed in a mustard vinaigrette would make a fine accompaniment to the croque-monsieurs.

HAM AND CHEESE TOPPING
4 tablespoons (½ stick) unsalted butter
¼ cup all-purpose flour
2 cups whole milk
1 teaspoon salt
1 teaspoon freshly grated nutmeg, divided
2 pinches plus ¼ teaspoon Cayenne pepper, divided
10 ounces Gruyère cheese (4 ounces grated plus 6 ounces thinly sliced)
6 ounces thinly sliced ham, preferably Black Forest
2 to 3 teaspoons chopped fresh Italian parsley (optional)

1 recipe Best-Ever Classic Waffles (page 33), prepared without sugar

➤ To make the Ham and Cheese Topping: Melt the butter in a medium saucepan over medium heat. Add the flour and stir 1 minute. Whisk in the milk, salt, ¼ teaspoon of the nutmeg, and a couple pinches of the cayenne. Whisk constantly until the sauce thickens, 1 to 2 minutes. Remove from the heat and cover to keep warm. Mix the grated Gruyère, the remaining ¾ teaspoon nutmeg, and ¼ teaspoon cayenne in a bowl and set aside. Have the sliced cheese and ham ready to use.

➤ To assemble the Croque-Monsieur Waffles: Prepare the waffles according to directions. Arrange an oven rack 4 to 5 inches from the broiler. Line a large baking sheet with aluminum foil and put 6 waffles on the sheet. (Save extra waffles for another use.) Top each waffle with some sliced cheese, then with some sliced ham. Spread some sauce over each waffle, then sprinkle with the grated Gruyère mixture.

➤ Place the waffles under the broiler until the cheese melts and begins to bubble, 1 minute or more. Watch carefully so that the waffles do not burn. Remove them and use a spatula to transfer a waffle to each of 6 dinner plates. Sprinkle each serving with the parsley, if desired.

SERVES 6

Southwest Waffles with Avocado Salsa

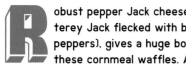obust pepper Jack cheese (a variety of Monterey Jack flecked with bits of hot chile peppers), gives a huge boost of flavor to these cornmeal waffles. As the batter bakes, the cheese melts and imparts a spicy accent. These crisp, golden brown waffles, garnished with a vibrant green avocado salsa, would make a fine brunch entrée accompanied by a salad of mixed greens and fresh orange segments tossed in a vinaigrette dressing.

TOPPING
• Avocado Salsa (page 90)

SOUTHWEST WAFFLES
1½ cups all-purpose flour
⅔ cup grated pepper Jack cheese
½ cup yellow cornmeal (Use regular, not coarsely ground, cornmeal.)
2 teaspoons baking powder
1½ teaspoons ground cumin
¼ teaspoon baking soda
¼ teaspoon salt
2 cups reduced fat or nonfat buttermilk
2 large eggs, separated
4 tablespoons (½ stick) unsalted butter, melted and slightly cooled

➤ Prepare the Avocado Salsa according to the directions and set aside.

➤ To make the Southwest Waffles: Preheat a waffle iron, and if you plan to hold the waffles until serving time, preheat the oven to 200°F.

➤ In a large bowl, stir together the flour, cheese, cornmeal, baking powder, cumin, baking soda, and salt. In another bowl, whisk together the buttermilk and egg yolks until completely blended. In a small bowl, beat the egg whites until firm, but not stiff.

➤ Make a well in the dry ingredients and pour in the milk/egg mixture, blending gently only until the ingredients are combined. Add the butter in a slow stream, continuing to blend until the butter is incorporated. Gently fold in the egg whites.

➤ Pour a generous ½ cup batter (or more, depending on the size of your waffle iron) into the waffle iron and, using a metal spatula or table knife, spread batter to within ½ inch of the edge. Close the cover, and cook approximately 3 minutes, or until crisp and golden brown. Serve the waffles immediately, or place them in a single layer on racks in the preheated oven while you finish with the remaining batter.

➤ To serve, arrange a waffle on each of 6 dinner plates. (Save extra waffles for another use.) Serve the waffles with a generous dollop of Avocado Salsa.

SERVES 6

Orange Waffles with Figs, Goat Cheese, and Prosciutto

These extra-light, orange-scented waffles are a perfect canvas for a topping of fresh figs, bits of creamy goat cheese, and crisp, panfried strips of prosciutto. The sweetness of the orange and figs melds admirably with the salty accent of the cheese and ham. Serve these for a light lunch with a mixed green salad.

TOPPINGS

1 tablespoon unsalted butter
3 ounces thinly sliced prosciutto, cut into julienne strips about ¼ inch by 3 inches
12 medium fresh figs (about 9 ounces)
4 ounces creamy goat cheese, broken into small bits
1 tablespoon chopped fresh Italian parsley, plus 6 fresh parsley sprigs
Julienned orange peel for garnish (optional, see Note)

ORANGE WAFFLES

1½ cups all-purpose flour
4 teaspoons baking powder
½ teaspoon salt
¼ teaspoon baking soda
1¾ cups freshly squeezed orange juice (or premium store-bought)
2 large eggs, separated
4 teaspoons grated orange zest
6 tablespoons (¾ stick) unsalted butter, melted and slightly cooled

➤ To make the Toppings: Melt the butter in a large skillet over medium-high heat. When hot, add the prosciutto and cook, stirring, until crisp, 3 to 4 minutes. Remove and drain on paper towels. Slice each fig into 4 slices and set aside.

➤ To make the Orange Waffles: Preheat a waffle iron, and if you plan to hold the waffles until serving time, preheat the oven to 200°F.

➤ In a large bowl, stir together the flour, baking powder, salt, and baking soda. In another bowl, whisk together the orange juice and egg yolks until completely blended. In a small bowl, beat the egg whites until firm, but not stiff.

➤ Make a well in the dry ingredients and pour in the orange juice/egg mixture, blending gently only until the ingredients are combined. Stir the orange zest into the butter, then add the butter in a slow stream, continuing to blend until the butter is incorporated. Gently fold in the egg whites. The batter may be thinner than usual.

➤ Pour a generous ½ cup batter (or more, depending on the size of your waffle iron) into the waffle iron and, using a metal spatula or table knife, spread batter to within ½ inch of the edge. Close the cover, and cook approximately 3 minutes, or until crisp and golden brown. Serve the waffles immediately, or place them them in a single layer on racks in the preheated oven while you finish with the remaining batter.

➤ To serve, arrange a waffle on each of 6 dinner plates. (Save extra waffles for another use.) Garnish each waffle with the sliced figs, bits of goat cheese, and crumbled prosciutto. Sprinkle each serving with the parsley and garnish with a parsley sprig. If desired, add a few orange strips.

SERVES 6

 NOTE: For julienned orange strips, use a citrus stripper or peel an orange with a vegetable peeler, avoiding the white pith beneath the skin. Cut the strips into thin julienne strips about ¼ inch by 3 inches.

CHAPTER III

Great Finales—

Dessert Waffles

Sweet waffles can easily step onto the dessert stage. Use them as a grand finale to a supper or give them a starring role at a dessert party. Dessert flavorings adapt beautifully to waffles.

Chocolate, the world's favorite sweet taste, is featured in more than one recipe in this chapter. There are Chocolate Waffles, made with a batter that calls for both cocoa powder and grated chocolate. The dark brown waffles are topped with scoops of coffee ice cream, then drizzled with warm chocolate sauce. Another entry sure to please chocoholics is Chocolate Chip–Pecan Waffles, which are studded with mini chocolate chips and chopped nuts.

Dessert waffles pair well with berries and other fruits. Raised Belgian Waffles, made with a yeasted batter and baked in a special waffle iron with deep grids, are garnished with fresh strawberries and whipped cream. Blueberries, raspberries, and blackberries are incorporated into a buttermilk batter in Very Berry Waffles, while sliced bananas paired with vanilla ice cream and warm caramel sauce serve as a topping for Bananas Foster Waffles.

Shredded coconut flakes and coconut milk impart a delicious taste to Coconut Waffles, and ground ginger and molasses provide the robust seasonings for Gingerbread Waffles.

You can even turn leftover sweet waffles into scrumptious desserts. Extra waffles can be cut into small squares, crisped in the oven, then used to make Warm Waffle "Bread" Pudding or Waffle Trifle with Raspberries. And, you'll find a recipe for thin waffle cookies called pizzelle. These are baked in a pizzelle maker, a type of waffle press with thin decorative molds.

Cole Porter's words describe the waffles in this chapter best: "They're delightful, they're delicious, they're de-lovely!" They're dessert!

Raised Belgian Waffles

Belgian waffles made their earliest appearance on this side of the Atlantic during the World's Fair in New York in 1964. Made in waffle irons with deeper than usual grids, Belgian waffles are taller and statelier than other waffles. Although some recipes for these waffles do not call for yeast, raised ones have an old-fashioned charm and a distinctive taste. My assistant, Deb Brown, created the delicious version that follows. Strawberries and whipped cream are the most popular garnish, but Dark Chocolate Sauce or Nutella, a luscious spread of hazelnuts and chocolate available in most groceries, are other tempting embellishments.

2 cups milk
8 tablespoons (1 stick) unsalted butter, diced
2 cups all-purpose flour
4 teaspoons sugar
1½ teaspoons instant yeast (Rapid Rise works well.)
½ teaspoon salt
2 large eggs
1 teaspoon vanilla extract

TOPPINGS
• 4 cups fresh strawberries, sliced; and 1 cup heavy (whipping) cream, whipped until firm and sweetened with 2 teaspoons confectioners' sugar
• Dark Chocolate Sauce (page 78)
• Nutella
Confectioners' sugar (for dusting)

➤ Twelve to 24 hours ahead: Whisk or stir the milk and butter in a medium saucepan over medium heat until the butter is just melted and an instant-read thermometer registers 120° to 130°F. Set aside.

➤ In a large bowl, stir together the flour, sugar, yeast, and salt. In a medium bowl, beat the eggs with the vanilla. Make a well in the dry ingredients and pour in the milk/butter mixture in a slow stream, blending gently with a whisk or fork. The mixture will be quite lumpy. Add the egg mixture, blending just until incorporated. Cover with plastic wrap and put in the refrigerator for 12 to 24 hours.

➤ When ready to cook the waffles: Preheat a waffle iron (preferably a Belgian waffle iron), and if you plan to hold the waffles until serving time, preheat the oven to 200°F.

➤ Using a whisk, gently stir the batter (which will have doubled in size while resting in the refrigerator) to blend all the ingredients. The batter will deflate.

➤ Scoop a generous ½ cup batter (or more, depending on the size of your waffle iron) into the waffle iron and, using a metal spatula or table knife, spread batter to within ½ inch of the edge. Close the cover, and cook approximately 3 minutes, or until crisp and golden brown. Serve the waffles immediately, or place them in a single layer on racks in the preheated oven while you finish with the remaining batter.

➤ Serve the waffles with the topping of your choice. Dust with confectioners' sugar.

MAKES 6 OR MORE 6½-INCH WAFFLES; SERVES 4 TO 6

Gingerbread Waffles with Vanilla Ice Cream and Warm Lemon Sauce

The enticing aroma of these dark brown waffles scented with ginger brings back childhood memories of comfort food served on cold days. In this recipe it's not cake, but rather scrumptious waffles, prepared with dark thick molasses, that draws people to the table. Topped with vanilla ice cream and napped with Warm Lemon Sauce, these waffles please young and old alike.

1¾ cups all-purpose flour
½ cup sugar
2 teaspoons ground ginger
1 teaspoon salt
1 teaspoon baking powder
½ teaspoon baking soda
2 large eggs
½ cup unsulphured molasses (see Note)
⅔ cup milk
8 tablespoons (1 stick) unsalted butter, melted and slightly cooled

TOPPING
• 1 pint best-quality vanilla ice cream; Warm Lemon Sauce (page 77); 6 fresh mint sprigs (optional); and 6 thin julienned lemon strips, about ¼ inch by 3 inches (see Note page 53; optional)

➤ Heat a waffle iron, and have ready 2 cooling racks on a work surface.

➤ In a large bowl, sift together the flour, sugar, ginger, salt, baking powder, and baking soda. In another bowl, beat the eggs to blend and then whisk in the molasses.

➤ Make a well in the dry ingredients and pour in the egg/molasses mixture, stirring until the liquid is absorbed. (The batter will be very thick at this point.). Whisk together the milk and butter in another bowl, then stir this mixture into the batter, blending gently only until the ingredients are combined.

➤ Pour a generous ½ cup batter (or more, depending on the size of your waffle iron) into the waffle iron and, using a metal spatula or table knife, spread batter to within ½ inch of the edge. Close the cover, and cook approximately 3 minutes, or until the waffle is set. This waffle will have a cakelike (not a crisp) texture when done. Place the waffles on cooling racks while you finish with the remaining batter. While cooling, the waffles will become crisp on the outside.

➤ Serve the waffles with 1 or 2 scoops of vanilla ice cream. Drizzle Warm Lemon Sauce over each serving and garnish each with a sprig of mint and a lemon strip, if desired.

MAKES 6 OR MORE 6½-INCH WAFFLES; SERVES 4 TO 6

NOTE: Both sulphured and unsulphured molasses are available. The latter is lighter and has a cleaner flavor.

Chocolate Chip–Pecan Waffles with Vanilla Ice Cream and Dark Chocolate Sauce

hocolate chip cookie fans will love these sweet waffles studded with small bits of chocolate and chopped pecans. Serve the warm waffles with scoops of vanilla ice cream and a drizzle of warm Dark Chocolate Sauce. Mini chocolate chips, available in the baking section of most groceries, work best in this recipe.

1½ cups all-purpose flour
6 tablespoons chopped, toasted pecans (see Note page 29)
3 tablespoons packed light brown sugar
2 teaspoons baking powder
Pinch salt
1 cup milk
2 large eggs, separated
2 teaspoons vanilla extract
4 tablespoons (½ stick) unsalted butter, melted and slightly cooled
6 tablespoons mini chocolate chips

TOPPING
• 1 pint best-quality vanilla ice cream; Dark Chocolate Sauce (page 78), with Kahlúa or rum omitted

➤ Preheat a waffle iron, and if you plan to hold the waffles until serving time, preheat the oven to 200°F.

➤ In a large bowl, stir together the flour, pecans, brown sugar, baking powder, and salt. In a medium bowl, whisk together the milk, egg yolks, and vanilla until completely blended. In a small bowl, beat the egg whites until firm, but not stiff.

➤ Make a well in the dry ingredients and pour in the milk/egg mixture, blending gently only until the ingredients are combined. Add the butter in a slow stream, continuing to blend until the butter is incorporated. Gently fold in the egg whites and chocolate chips.

➤ Pour a generous ½ cup batter (or more, depending on the size of your waffle iron) into the waffle iron and, using a metal spatula or table knife, spread batter to within ½ inch of the edge. (This batter will be thick.) Close the cover, and cook approximately 3 minutes, or until crisp and golden brown. Serve the waffles immediately, or place them in a single layer on racks in the preheated oven while you finish with the remaining batter.

➤ Serve the waffles topped with 1 or 2 scoops of vanilla ice cream and a drizzle of Dark Chocolate Sauce.

MAKES 6 OR MORE 6½-INCH WAFFLES; SERVES 4 TO 6

Chocolate Waffles with Coffee Ice Cream and Dark Chocolate Sauce

hocolate and coffee, a winning flavor combination, star in this dessert. Rich, dense chocolate waffles made with two types of chocolate (cocoa powder and grated chocolate) are topped with scoops of coffee ice cream, then drizzled with warm decadent Dark Chocolate Sauce. The waffles can be made in advance and reheated at serving time.

1½ cups all-purpose flour
½ cup granulated sugar
½ cup unsweetened cocoa powder
3 ounces unsweetened chocolate, grated or chopped in a food processor
2 tablespoons packed light brown sugar
2 teaspoons baking powder
¼ teaspoon baking soda
¼ teaspoon salt
1½ cups milk
2 large eggs, separated
1 teaspoon vanilla extract
6 tablespoons (¾ stick) unsalted butter, melted and slightly cooled

TOPPINGS
• 1 quart best-quality coffee ice cream, Dark Chocolate Sauce (page 78)
• 1 quart best-quality vanilla ice cream, Extra-Rich Caramel Sauce (page 77)

➤ Preheat a waffle iron, and if you plan to hold the waffles until serving time, preheat the oven to 200°F.

➤ In a large bowl, stir together the flour, granulated sugar, cocoa powder, grated chocolate, brown sugar, baking powder, baking soda, and salt. In another bowl, whisk together the milk, egg yolks, and vanilla until completely blended. In a small bowl, beat the egg whites until firm, but not stiff.

➤ Make a well in the dry ingredients and pour in the milk/egg mixture, blending gently only until the ingredients are combined. Add the butter in a slow stream, continuing to blend until the butter is incorporated. Gently fold in the egg whites.

➤ Pour a generous ½ cup batter (or more, depending on the size of your waffle iron) into the waffle iron and, using a metal spatula or table knife, spread batter to within ½ inch of the edge. Close the cover, and cook for approximately 3 minutes. The waffles will not be crisp, but will crisp up within a minute after they are removed from the waffle iron. Place the waffles in a single layer on racks in the preheated oven for no longer than 5 minutes (otherwise, they will dry out) to keep warm while you finish with the remaining batter.

➤ Serve the waffles with 1 or 2 scoops of coffee ice cream and a drizzle of Dark Chocolate Sauce.

MAKES 6 OR MORE 6½-INCH WAFFLES; SERVES 4 TO 6

Coconut Waffles

T oasted sweetened coconut flakes and coconut milk impart distinctive flavor to these waffles. Coconut pairs well with both chocolate and orange, so there are two equally tempting topping suggestions for these luscious waffles. Serve them with scoops of vanilla ice cream, a drizzle of warm Dark Chocolate Sauce, and a sprinkle of toasted coconut flakes. Or, offer them with Orange Ambrosia, a mélange of fresh oranges, toasted almonds, and coconut flakes, and softly whipped cream. Either way, they make a mouthwatering dessert for a special occasion.

1½ cups all-purpose flour
1 cup toasted sweetened coconut flakes (see Note)
2 tablespoons sugar
2 teaspoons baking powder
¼ teaspoon salt
One 14-ounce can coconut milk
2 large eggs
½ teaspoon vanilla extract
6 tablespoons (¾ stick) unsalted butter, melted and slightly cooled

TOPPINGS
• 1 pint best-quality vanilla ice cream; Dark Chocolate Sauce (page 78); ½ cup toasted sweetened coconut flakes (see Note); Confectioners' sugar
• Orange Ambrosia (page 90); 1 cup heavy (whipping) cream, whipped until firm and sweetened with 2 teaspoons confectioners' sugar

➤ Preheat a waffle iron, and if you plan to hold the waffles until serving time, preheat the oven to 200°F.

➤ In a large bowl, stir together the flour, coconut flakes, sugar, baking powder, and salt. In a medium bowl, whisk together the coconut milk, eggs, and vanilla until completely blended.

➤ Make a well in the dry ingredients and pour in the coconut milk/egg mixture, blending gently only until the ingredients are combined. Add the butter in a slow stream, continuing to blend until the butter is incorporated.

➤ Pour a generous ½ cup batter (or more, depending on the size of your waffle iron) into the waffle iron and, using a metal spatula or table knife, spread batter to within ½ inch of the edge. Close the cover, and cook approximately 3 minutes, or until crisp and golden brown. Serve the waffles immediately, or place them in a single layer on racks in the preheated oven while you finish with the remaining batter.

➤ Serve the waffles with the topping of your choice.

MAKES 6 OR MORE 6½-INCH WAFFLES; SERVES 4 TO 6

 NOTE: To toast sweetened coconut flakes: Arrange an oven rack at center position and preheat the oven to 350°F. Spread the coconut flakes on a baking sheet with sides, and bake until the flakes just start to brown, 4 to 5 minutes. Watch carefully, as coconut flakes brown very quickly. Remove them from the oven, transfer to a plate, and cool.

Warm Waffle "Bread" Pudding

Sweet waffles easily replace bread in this scrumptious variation of a classic bread pudding. Crisp oven-toasted waffle squares are combined with raisins, then covered with a vanilla-scented custard. The baked pudding is irresistible accompanied by Extra-Rich Caramel Sauce, sweetened whipped cream, or vanilla ice cream. Leftover waffles are perfect for this pudding.

1 teaspoon butter
4½ cups cubed sweet waffles (1-inch squares; see Note)
½ cup raisins
2 large eggs plus 3 large egg yolks
¼ cup sugar
1¾ cups milk
1½ cups heavy (whipping) cream
1 vanilla bean, split lengthwise

TOPPINGS
• Extra-Rich Caramel Sauce (page 77)
• 1 cup heavy (whipping) cream whipped until firm and sweetened with 1 tablespoon confectioners' sugar
• 1 pint best-quality vanilla ice cream
Confectioners' sugar (for dusting)

➤ Preheat the oven to 350°F. Butter an oven-to-table 2-quart baking dish.

➤ Spread the waffle pieces on a large baking sheet and bake them until crisp, 5 to 6 minutes. Remove them from the oven and cool, then spread them in the prepared dish. Sprinkle the raisins over the top.

➤ Put the eggs and egg yolks in a medium, heavy saucepan and whisk in the sugar until well blended. Set aside.

➤ Put the milk, cream, and vanilla bean halves in a medium saucepan over medium-high heat. Heat until warm and small bubbles form around the edges of the pan, then remove it from the heat. With a fork or tongs, remove the vanilla bean halves and, using a sharp paring knife, scrape the pulp from each half into the milk mixture.

➤ In a thin stream, pour the milk into the egg mixture while whisking constantly. Place the saucepan over medium-low heat and whisk constantly until the mixture thickens slightly and coats the back of a spoon, 3 to 4 minutes or more. Remove the custard from the heat and pour it over the waffle pieces.

➤ Bake the pudding until set and golden on top, 20 to 25 minutes. Remove it from the oven and cool for 10 minutes.

➤ Dust the pudding with confectioners' sugar and serve with the topping of your choice.

SERVES 4 TO 6

NOTE: Three 6½-inch waffles will yield 4½ cups waffle squares. Sweet waffles such as Best-Ever Classic Waffles (page 33), Buttermilk Waffles (page 22), and Lighter Than Air Waffles (page 18) work well in this recipe.

Going Nuts Waffles

ust as the name implies, these waffles are loaded with nuts. A trio of nuts— hazelnuts, almonds, and pistachios—are included here. The nuts complement an orange-scented batter, adding extra crunch and texture. The nuts do not need to be toasted because they roast slightly in the waffle iron. The scrumptious waffles are heavenly served with dollops of Whipped Mascarpone Cream.

½ cup chopped hazelnuts
½ cup chopped slivered or sliced almonds
½ cup chopped unsalted pistachios
1½ cups all-purpose flour
4 teaspoons sugar
1 tablespoon baking powder
¼ teaspoon baking soda
¼ teaspoon salt
1 cup milk
1 cup freshly squeezed orange juice
2 large eggs, separated
1 tablespoon grated orange zest
6 tablespoons (¾ stick) unsalted butter, melted and
    slightly cooled

TOPPING
• Whipped Mascarpone Cream (page 85)

➤ Preheat a waffle iron, and if you plan to hold the waffles until serving time, preheat the oven to 200°F.

➤ Stir the nuts together in a medium bowl and set aside.

➤ In a large bowl, stir together 1 cup of the nuts, the flour, sugar, baking powder, baking soda, and salt. In a medium bowl, whisk together the milk, orange juice, and egg yolks until completely blended. In a small bowl, beat the egg whites until firm, but not stiff.

➤ Make a well in the dry ingredients and pour in the milk/egg mixture, blending gently only until the ingredients are combined. Stir the orange zest into the butter, then add the butter in a slow stream, continuing to blend until the butter is incorporated. Gently fold in the egg whites.

➤ Pour a generous ½ cup batter (or more, depending on the size of your waffle iron) into the waffle iron and, using a metal spatula or table knife, spread batter to within ½ inch of the edge. Close the cover, and cook approximately 3 minutes, or until crisp and golden brown. Serve the waffles immediately, or place them in a single layer on racks in the preheated oven while you finish with the remaining batter.

➤ Serve the waffles with a generous dollop of Whipped Mascarpone Cream and a sprinkle of the remaining chopped nuts.

MAKES 6 OR MORE 6½-INCH WAFFLES; SERVES 4 TO 6

Very Berry Waffles

Good things come in threes, as in these waffles prepared with a trinity of summer berries. Raspberries, blueberries, and blackberries have starring roles in these sweet waffles. You can add the blueberries whole, but both the raspberries and blackberries will get more evenly distributed if they are cut into smaller pieces.

1½ cups fresh blueberries, divided
1½ cups fresh raspberries, divided
1 cup fresh blackberries, divided
1¾ cups all-purpose flour
4 teaspoons sugar
2 teaspoons baking powder
¼ teaspoon baking soda
¼ teaspoon salt
1¾ cups buttermilk
2 large eggs, separated
6 tablespoons (¾ stick) unsalted butter, melted and
    slightly cooled

TOPPING
• Orange-Scented Whipped Cream (page 83);
  Confectioners' sugar (for dusting); Fresh mint sprigs
  (optional)

➤ Preheat a waffle iron, and if you plan to hold the waffles until serving time, preheat the oven to 200°F.

➤ Put half of the blueberries in a bowl. Then cut half of the raspberries and half of the blackberries into small (½-inch) pieces. Add them to the bowl and toss gently to combine. Reserve the remaining berries for garnish.

➤ In a large bowl, stir together the flour, sugar, baking powder, baking soda, and salt. In another bowl, whisk together the buttermilk and egg yolks until completely blended. In a small bowl, beat the egg whites until firm, but not stiff.

➤ Make a well in the dry ingredients and pour in the milk/egg mixture, blending gently only until the ingredients are combined. Add the butter in a slow stream, continuing to blend until the butter is incorporated. Gently fold in the egg whites and then the prepared berries.

➤ Pour a generous ½ cup batter (or more, depending on the size of your waffle iron) into the waffle iron and, using a metal spatula or table knife, spread batter to within ½ inch of the edge. Close the cover, and cook approximately 3 minutes, or until crisp and golden brown. Serve the waffles immediately, or place them in a single layer on racks in the preheated oven while you finish with the remaining batter.

➤ Serve the waffles mounded with some of the remaining berries and topped with generous dollops of whipped cream. Dust with confectioners' sugar. Garnish each serving with a mint sprig, if desired.

MAKES 6 OR MORE 6½-INCH WAFFLES; SERVES 4 TO 6

Bananas Foster Waffles

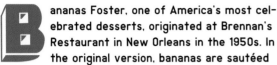**B**ananas Foster, one of America's most celebrated desserts, originated at Brennan's Restaurant in New Orleans in the 1950s. In the original version, bananas are sautéed in brown sugar, rum, and banana liqueur, then served with scoops of vanilla ice cream. This all-time favorite gets a new twist in the following recipe and becomes a delectable topping for crisp golden waffles.

1 recipe Best-Ever Classic Waffles (page 33) or Lighter Than Air Waffles (page 18)

TOPPING
1 double recipe Extra-Rich Caramel Sauce (page 77; see Note)
3 to 4 tablespoons dark rum
3 ripe medium bananas
1 pint best-quality vanilla ice cream
½ cup toasted pecans, coarsely chopped (see Note page 29)
6 fresh mint sprigs (optional)

➤ Prepare the waffles according to directions and keep warm in a single layer on racks in a 200°F oven.

➤ Prepare the Extra-Rich Caramel Sauce and, while still warm, remove it from the heat and stir in 3 tablespoons rum (or 4 for a more pronounced taste). Slice the bananas, crosswise, into thin rounds.

➤ Serve the waffles with 1 or 2 scoops of vanilla ice cream, and garnish with some sliced bananas. Drizzle each serving with warm Caramel Sauce and sprinkle with the pecans. Garnish each plate with a mint sprig, if desired.

MAKES 6 OR MORE 6½-INCH WAFFLES; SERVES 4 TO 6

NOTE: These waffles are easier to assemble if you make the Extra-Rich Caramel Sauce in advance. Refrigerate the sauce, covered, for up to 5 days.

Waffle Trifle with Raspberries

Sweet waffles can be turned into a delicious trifle, a classic English dessert made by drenching ladyfingers or sponge cake in sherry, then adding fruit, whipped cream, and custard. In this version, waffles are cut into squares, crisped in the oven, then soaked in sherry. They are topped with raspberry jam and fresh raspberries, then with a spiced whipped cream layer, and finally with a custard sauce. It's worth noting that leftover waffles work beautifully in this recipe.

1½ recipes Spiced Honey Whipped Cream (page 84)
2½ cups cubed sweet waffles (1-inch squares; see Note)
5 tablespoons dry sherry
¼ cup raspberry jam
2½ cups (12 ounces) fresh raspberries, plus 3 to 4 raspberries for garnish
5 large egg yolks
¼ cup sugar
2 cups whole milk
½ cup toasted sliced almonds (optional; see Note page 29)

➤ Have ready a large 2- to 3-quart serving bowl. Preheat the oven to 350°F.

➤ Prepare the Spiced Honey Whipped Cream according to directions; cover and refrigerate.

➤ Spread the waffle pieces on a large baking sheet and bake until crisp, 5 to 6 minutes. Remove them from the oven and cool. Arrange the pieces in the bowl in a single layer, covering the bottom and going partway up the sides. Drizzle them with the sherry. Drop teaspoonfuls of the jam over the waffles, then top with the 2½ cups raspberries. Spread the Spiced Honey Whipped Cream over the raspberries. Cover the bowl and refrigerate.

➤ Put the egg yolks in a medium bowl, and gradually whisk in the sugar until blended. Heat the milk in a medium, heavy saucepan over medium heat until warm, but not hot. Slowly pour the milk over the egg mixture, while whisking to combine. Pour the egg mixture back into the saucepan and place it over medium heat. Stir constantly until the sauce thickens and coats the back of a spoon, 3 minutes or longer. (Lower the heat if necessary so that the mixture does not come to a boil and curdle.) Transfer the custard to a heat-proof bowl and refrigerate (uncovered to prevent condensation) until chilled but not set. Then pour the custard over the whipped cream layer in the bowl.

➤ Cover the trifle and refrigerate it for 6 hours or overnight to allow the flavors to meld.

➤ To serve, garnish the trifle with the reserved raspberries and, if desired, sprinkle it with the almonds.

SERVES 6 TO 8

NOTE: One and a half 6½-inch waffles will yield 2½ cups squares. Sweet waffles, such as Best-Ever Classic Waffles (page 33), Buttermilk Waffles (page 22), or Lighter Than Air Waffles (page 18), work well in this recipe.

Pizzelle (Italian Waffle Cookies)

The paper-thin, Italian wafer cookies known as pizzelle are popular the world over. To make them, a vanilla- or anise-scented batter is poured into a pizzelle maker (a type of shallow waffle press with round patterned molds), then quickly baked until golden. The cookies crisp as they cool on racks. Pizzelle can also be fashioned into cups, cones, or cannoli when shaped the second they are removed from the press.

1 cup all-purpose flour
¾ teaspoon baking powder
5 tablespoons unsalted butter, melted and slightly cooled
2 teaspoons vanilla or anise extract
2 large eggs
½ cup sugar
Vegetable oil (optional; see recipe)

➤ Preheat a pizzelle press. Have ready 1 or 2 cooling racks.

➤ Combine the flour and baking powder in a medium bowl and set aside. In another bowl, combine the butter and vanilla and set aside.

➤ Put the eggs and sugar in a large bowl. With an electric mixer on medium speed, beat until smooth and thickened, about 1 minute. Reduce the speed to low, and add the butter and vanilla, beating only 15 to 20 seconds to blend. Then add all the flour mixture and beat just until combined, 10 to 15 seconds more. Be careful not to overmix.

➤ Follow the manufacturer's guidelines for preparing the pizzelle maker. (Some suggest brushing the top and bottom grids of the molds lightly with an unflavored vegetable oil, not butter or nonstick spray, to prevent sticking.) Spoon the batter into the pizzelle mold. For 3½-inch molds, you'll need a heaping teaspoon, for 6½- to 7-inch molds, you'll need about 1 tablespoon.

➤ Bake until golden, usually about 4 minutes. Remove the pizzelle and cool them on racks. Store the cookies in an airtight container at room temperature for up to 1 week.

MAKES 18 TO 20 SMALL (3½-INCH) PIZZELLE

 VARIATION: These cookies are delicious when spread on 1 side with some warm Dark Chocolate Sauce (page 78). Set them on a baking sheet and refrigerate until the chocolate is set. Then store in an airtight container in the refrigerator.

Pizzelle Ice Cream Sandwiches

Pizzelle can be turned into delectable ice cream sandwiches. Coat the cookies with some Dark Chocolate Sauce, spread softened vanilla ice cream on one cookie, and gently press a second cookie on top. This is a great project for aspiring young chefs to enjoy with parents in the kitchen.

> 1 recipe Dark Chocolate Sauce (page 78), made with-
>   out Kahlúa or rum
> 12 small (3½- to 4-inch) pizzelle (facing page)
> 1 quart best-quality vanilla ice cream, softened slightly

➤ Prepare the Dark Chocolate Sauce according to directions and heat it over medium-low heat, stirring until warm and smooth. With a spoon, spread 1 side of each of the cookies with about 2 teaspoons of the sauce. (You will probably have some sauce left over; save for another use.) As the cookies are spread with chocolate, put them, chocolate sides up, on a rack. Cool until the chocolate is set.

➤ To make a sandwich, scoop 2 or 3 small balls of vanilla ice cream onto the chocolate side of 1 of the cookies. Gently pat the ice cream flat with a spatula or table knife. Carefully, top with a second cookie, chocolate side down, and press very gently. As each sandwich is made, transfer it to the freezer. When all the sandwiches have been assembled, you can store them in a single large lock-top plastic bag, or in individual ones. (The sandwiches can be prepared 1 day ahead.)

MAKES SIX 3½- TO 4-INCH SANDWICHES; SERVES 6

TO SHAPE PIZZELLE INTO CUPS, CONES, OR CANNOLI:
➤ Large 6½- to 7-inch pizzelle are easier to shape.
➤ Shape the pizzelle into the desired form the instant it comes off the press since it will harden within seconds.
➤ To make cups, have ready 1-cup ramekins, soufflés, or custard cups. Mold the pizzelle inside the cup to form a bowl shape. (Most recipes have you mold on the outside, but the inside produces a more attractive cup.)
➤ To make cones, shape a pizzelle around a wooden or plastic cone, available in cookware stores, and gently flatten the seam together with your fingers.
➤ To make cannoli, roll pizzelle around a wooden dowel about 1 inch in diameter and gently flatten the seam together with your fingers.

CHAPTER IV

Gilding the Lily—Waffle Toppings

You can dress up any waffle — sweet or savory — with a complementary topping. I think of these toppings as smart accessories that complete a look. Most cooks reach for butter and maple syrup when serving breakfast waffles, but there are many more options. For example, pats of Orange-Honey Butter or Pecan Toffee Crunch Butter spread on piping hot waffles will add incredible flavor. And, in place of maple syrup, try beautiful crimson Cranberry Syrup or spiced Cider Syrup for a change.

Fruit sauces and fruit compotes are winning partners to both breakfast and dessert waffles. Let the season determine which fruit you use. In summer, you might choose one of the berry sauces — Night Before Blueberry Sauce, Summertime Strawberry Sauce, or Smooth as Silk Raspberry Glaze — to drizzle over breakfast or dessert waffles. In colder months, you'll be tempted by Apricot-Cherry Compote (made with dried fruits), Cranberry-Apple Compote, and Orange Ambrosia. All-time favorites — chocolate, caramel, and warm lemon sauces — pair well with breakfast or dessert waffles any day of the year.

For festive occasions, you can top sweet waffles with glorious whipped creams flavored with spirits and spices. Whipped Maple Cream makes a perfect partner to Pumpkin Waffles; Lemon Chantilly Cream adds panache to Lemon Poppy Seed Waffles; and Whipped Mascarpone Cream looks beautiful atop Going Nuts Waffles.

For savory waffles, there are salsas and a chutney to choose from. Avocado Salsa, for example, crowns Southwest Waffles (made with cornmeal and grated pepper Jack cheese), turning them into real crowd pleasers. Fresh Tomato and Yellow Pepper Salsa does the same for Corn Waffles, while warm homemade Plum Chutney enhances the flavors in the Indian Spiced Waffles.

These toppings will take a few extra minutes to prepare, but will yield great dividends. They add bursts of flavor, color, and splendor to a dish of waffles.

Sweet Sauces, Glazes, and Butters

Summertime Strawberry Sauce

This sauce is best made when strawberries are at their peak and bursting with flavor. They should be red-hued to their cores and juicy. In this recipe half the berries are crushed with sugar, then simmered in orange juice along with some cornstarch until thickened. Then the remaining berries are sliced and stirred in. Try this colorful garnish with Best-Ever Classic Waffles (page 33), Buttermilk Waffles (page 22), or Lighter Than Air Waffles (page 18).

3 cups (1½ pints) fresh strawberries, hulled
4 to 5 tablespoons sugar
¼ cup freshly squeezed orange juice, plus more if needed
1 teaspoon cornstarch
½ teaspoon grated orange zest

➤ Thinly slice half of the strawberries and put them in a heavy, medium saucepan. Add 4 tablespoons of sugar, the orange juice, cornstarch, and orange zest. With a potato masher, a meat pounder, or a wooden spoon, crush the berries well. Place the pan over medium heat and stir until the sugar has dissolved. Continue to cook, stirring, until the mixture thickens, 4 minutes or less.

➤ Remove the pan from the heat. Taste and, if desired, stir in the remaining 1 tablespoon of sugar. (The sauce can be prepared 1 day ahead to this point; cool, cover, and refrigerate. Reheat, stirring, when ready to use.)

➤ To finish the sauce, slice the remaining berries and stir them into the warm sauce. If the sauce is too thick, thin it with additional orange juice.

MAKES 2 CUPS

Night Before
Blueberry Sauce

A flavorful sauce makes a fine partner to Double Blueberry Waffles (page 27), Best-Ever Classic Waffles (page 33), Buttermilk Waffles (page 22), or Lemon Poppy Seed Waffles (page 24), as well as to Waffled French Toasts (page 34).

½ cup sugar
3 tablespoons freshly squeezed lemon juice
2 tablespoons cornstarch
1½ cups fresh or frozen blueberries
¼ teaspoon ground cinnamon
⅛ teaspoon freshly grated nutmeg

➤ In a medium saucepan, stir together 1 cup water (see Note), the sugar, lemon juice, and cornstarch.

➤ Place the pan over medium-high heat and cook, stirring until the cornstarch dissolves and the mixture boils. Add the blueberries and boil, stirring constantly, until the sauce thickens enough to coat the back of a wooden spoon, 6 to 8 minutes or longer. Remove the sauce from the heat and cool for 10 minutes. Stir in the cinnamon and nutmeg. (The sauce can be prepared 2 days ahead; cool, cover and refrigerate. Reheat, stirring, over medium heat.)

MAKES ABOUT 2 CUPS

NOTE: For a variation, use ½ cup each water and red wine. The wine adds an extra note of tartness that acts as a counterpoint to the sugar in the sauce.

Smooth as Silk
Raspberry Glaze

T his deep red, silken smooth sauce (pictured on page 74) takes only minutes to assemble and can be prepared in advance. It's a fabulous complement to Best-Ever Classic Waffles (page 33), Lighter Than Air Waffles (page 18), or Buttermilk Waffles (page 22), and is equally tempting as a garnish for Waffled French Toasts (page 34).

2 cups (1 pint) fresh raspberries
¼ cup sugar, plus more if needed
2 tablespoons freshly squeezed lemon juice

➤ Put the berries, sugar, and lemon juice in a food processor fitted with the metal blade or in a blender. Process, pulsing the machine, until puréed. Using a fine-mesh sieve, strain the berries to remove the seeds. Taste, and if the mixture is too tart, stir in additional sugar.

➤ Heat the sauce in a small saucepan over medium heat until just warm. (The sauce can be prepared 3 days ahead; cool, cover, and refrigerate. Reheat, stirring, over low heat until just warm.)

MAKES ABOUT 1 CUP

Warm Lemon Sauce

The bright clear taste of lemon shines through in this sauce, which can be prepared in advance and reheated at serving time. It's irresistible when served over Gingerbread Waffles (page 58) topped with scoops of vanilla ice cream. Try it too with Very Berry Waffles (page 65).

¾ cup sugar
3 tablespoons cornstarch
⅛ teaspoon salt
4½ tablespoons freshly squeezed lemon juice
3 tablespoons unsalted butter, diced
1 tablespoon grated lemon zest
2 large egg yolks

➤ Combine the sugar, cornstarch, and salt in a heavy, nonreactive, medium saucepan. Whisk in 1½ cups water until blended. Place the pan over medium heat and cook, whisking constantly, until the sauce is clear and thick.

➤ Remove the pan from the heat and stir in the lemon juice, butter, and lemon zest. Put the egg yolks in a small bowl, and slowly whisk in ½ cup of the warm sauce. Whisk the egg mixture back into the pan with the warm sauce. Heat the sauce again, whisking constantly over low heat until it thickens a little more, about 1 minute. (The sauce can be prepared 2 days ahead; cool, cover, and refrigerate. Reheat over low heat, stirring constantly. If the sauce is too thick after reheating, thin it with 2 to 3 tablespoons water.)

MAKES ABOUT 1½ CUPS

Extra-Rich Caramel Sauce

Only four ingredients plus water are needed to make this unbelievably rich and velvety smooth caramel sauce. The sauce keeps well for several days in the refrigerator and is particularly good on Bananas Foster Waffles (page 66) and Warm Waffle "Bread" Pudding (page 63).

1 cup sugar
½ cup half-and-half or light cream
3 tablespoons unsalted butter, diced
2 tablespoons sour cream

➤ Put the sugar and ½ cup water in a heavy, medium saucepan over low heat, swirling the pan occasionally until the sugar dissolves. Increase the heat and boil until the syrup turns a rich golden brown color, 6 to 8 minutes.

➤ Remove the pan from the heat and stir in the half-and-half and butter. Be very careful, averting your face, since the mixture will bubble vigorously. Stir or whisk it until the mixture is smooth. Whisk in the sour cream. (The sauce can be prepared 5 days ahead; cool, cover, and refrigerate. Reheat over medium heat, stirring constantly.)

MAKES ABOUT 1 CUP

Dark Chocolate Sauce

This dark chocolate sauce calls for only three ingredients: cream, chocolate, and coffee. If you want to enliven this mixture, you can stir in a couple of tablespoons of coffee liqueur or dark rum. This rich warm sauce makes good things even better—use it to embellish Raised Belgian Waffles (page 57), Chocolate Waffles (page 60), Chocolate Chip–Pecan Waffles (page 59), or any waffle you think would pair well with chocolate.

> 1 cup heavy (whipping) cream
> 8 ounces semisweet chocolate, coarsely chopped
> ½ teaspoon instant coffee powder
> 2 tablespoons Kahlúa or dark rum (optional)

➤ Heat the cream in a heavy saucepan over medium-high heat until hot. Reduce the heat to low and add the chocolate and coffee powder. Whisk until smooth and shiny. Remove the sauce from the heat and stir in the liquor, if desired. (The sauce can be prepared 5 days ahead; cool, cover, and refrigerate. Reheat, stirring, over medium-low heat.)

MAKES 1½ CUPS

Orange-Honey Butter

Here's a luscious topping, made by blending together softened butter, orange marmalade, and honey, that can be prepared in advance and stored in the refrigerator. It is especially good with Whole Wheat Waffles (page 21) and with Multigrain Extravaganza Waffles (page 23).

> 6 tablespoons (¾ stick) unsalted butter, at room temperature
> 3 tablespoons orange marmalade
> 1½ teaspoons honey

➤ Put all the ingredients in a bowl and mix well. Transfer the mixture to a small serving bowl or ramekin. Cover and refrigerate if not using immediately. (The butter can be prepared up to 2 days ahead; bring it to room temperature 30 minutes before using.)

MAKES ABOUT ½ CUP

Pecan Toffee Crunch Butter

To make this sublime butter, chopped pecans, toffee bits (available in the baking section of groceries), dark brown sugar, and butter are combined and spread on a baking sheet. After a few minutes in the oven, the toffee starts to melt and spread over the nuts. When cooled, the mixture hardens to a brittle, which is coarsely chopped and mixed with softened butter. This crunchy caramel butter complements all manner of waffles, in particular Whole Wheat Waffles (page 21), Pumpkin Waffles (page 29), or Banana Waffles (page 26).

Vegetable oil
½ cup pecans, toasted (see Note page 29)
⅓ cup toffee bits
2 teaspoons packed dark brown sugar
Generous pinch salt
1½ teaspoons unsalted butter, melted, plus 8 table-
    spoons (1 stick), slightly softened

➤ Arrange a rack at center position and preheat the oven to 350°F. Line a rimmed baking sheet with aluminum foil and grease it with the oil.

➤ Toss together the pecans, toffee bits, brown sugar, and salt in a medium bowl. Add the melted butter and toss again. Pat the mixture in the center of the baking sheet in a single layer. Bake until the toffee bits melt and spread, 4 to 5 minutes; watch carefully. Remove the pan from the oven and cool the mixture until it hardens.

➤ Gently lift the cooled toffee mixture off the foil onto a chopping board and, using a sharp knife, chop it coarsely. In a medium bowl, combine the chopped toffee mixture with the softened butter, mixing well until incorporated. Transfer the mixture to a small serving bowl. (The pecan toffee crunch mixture can be prepared 2 days ahead. Cover and leave it at cool room temperature.)

MAKES ABOUT 1¼ CUPS

Flavored Syrups and Whipped Creams

Cranberry Syrup

t's easy to turn cranberries into syrup. First, sugar is melted and liquefied in a saucepan, then cranberries, orange juice, and water are added. The cranberries, cooked until they pop, are strained out, then the cooking liquids are reduced until thickened. Drizzle this crimson-hued syrup over Best-Ever Classic Waffles (page 33) or any basic waffles. It makes a distinctive garnish to Holiday Waffles (page 32) and to Waffled French Toasts (page 34).

1⅓ cups sugar
3 cups (one 12-ounce package) frozen cranberries
1 cup freshly squeezed orange juice

➤ Put the sugar in a 4-quart heavy saucepan over medium heat. Cook without stirring until the sugar just begins to melt. Continue to cook, stirring occasionally with a fork, until the sugar has completely melted and is a rich golden brown.

➤ Carefully add the cranberries, orange juice, and 1 cup water to the pan. Avert your face as the mixture will release a lot of steam and bubble up. The sugar will solidify. Reduce the heat to low, and stir with a wooden spoon until the hardened sugar dissolves and the berries begin to pop, about 5 minutes. Remove the pan from the heat and carefully pour the syrup through a fine-mesh sieve set over a large bowl. Press hard with a spoon on the cranberries to release the juices. Discard the berries and return the syrup to the pan.

➤ Continue to simmer the syrup over low heat until thickened and reduced to about 1 cup, 8 to 10 minutes. (The syrup can be prepared 1 week ahead; cool, cover, and refrigerate. Reheat over low heat.)

MAKES 1 CUP

Cider Syrup

Amazingly, you can transform cider into a delicious syrup by cooking it with a small amount of sugar until the liquid has reduced and become thick. I add a cinnamon stick and lemon peel to round out the flavors. Try this rich golden syrup with Pumpkin Waffles (page 29) or Best-Ever Classic Waffles (page 33), or any basic waffle for a delectable change from traditional maple syrup.

6 cups cider
½ cup sugar
One 3-inch cinnamon stick, broken in half
One 3-inch strip lemon peel

➤ Combine the cider and sugar in a large (4- to 5-quart) saucepan set over high heat. Stir constantly with a wooden spoon until the sugar has dissolved. Add the cinnamon stick halves and lemon peel. Cook until the liquid has reduced to 1½ cups and is thickened and syrupy, 40 to 45 minutes. The cooking time will vary depending on the type of pan used and the intensity of the heat. Remove and discard the cinnamon halves and the lemon peel. (The syrup can be prepared 1 week ahead. Cool, cover, and refrigerate. Reheat over low heat, stirring occasionally.)

MAKES 1½ CUPS

Maple-Pecan Syrup

I live in New England, the maple syrup center of the universe, and as a result use this treasured sweetener, or liquid gold as some call it, in many different ways. For this recipe (pictured on page 81), I heat maple syrup and butter together, then stir in chopped toasted pecans. The syrup is especially good with Best-Ever Classic Waffles (page 33), Multigrain Extravaganza Waffles (page 23), Whole Wheat Waffles (page 21), or Banana Waffles (page 26).

1 cup maple syrup
4 tablespoons (½ stick) unsalted butter, diced
½ cup coarsely chopped toasted pecans (see Note page 29)

➤ Heat the maple syrup and butter in a medium, heavy saucepan over medium heat. When warm, stir in the pecans. Pour the syrup into a bowl or heat-proof pitcher and serve it with waffles. (The syrup can be prepared 1 day ahead; cool, cover, and refrigerate. Reheat over low heat.)

MAKES ABOUT 1⅓ CUPS

Orange-Scented Whipped Cream

Three-Minute Whipped Cream might be an even better name for this recipe, since it takes so little time to prepare. Orange liqueur and confectioners' sugar are all that are needed to transform ordinary whipped cream into a topping bursting with the refreshing taste of citrus. The cream is particularly good paired with fresh berries as a topping for Very Berry Waffles (page 65).

1 cup heavy (whipping) cream
2 tablespoons confectioners' sugar
4 teaspoons orange liqueur, such as Grand Marnier

➤ With an electric mixer on medium-high speed, whip the cream in a medium bowl until soft peaks form. Reduce the speed to low and add the sugar and orange liqueur. Continue beating until just firm. (The cream can be prepared 1 day ahead; cover and refrigerate. Whisk gently for a few seconds when ready to use.)

MAKES ABOUT 2 CUPS

Lemon Chantilly Cream

Purchased lemon curd plus extra lemon juice and zest are folded into whipped cream to produce this ethereally light topping. I love to serve it with Lemon Poppy Seed Waffles (page 24) along with a garnish of fresh blueberries, but you could also offer it with Very Berry Waffles (page 65) along with fresh blueberries, raspberries, or strawberries.

¾ cup heavy (whipping) cream
One 11-ounce jar lemon curd (see Note)
4 teaspoons freshly squeezed lemon juice
1 tablespoon grated lemon zest

➤ With an electric mixer on medium-high speed, whip the cream in a medium bowl until stiff peaks form. Mix together the lemon curd, juice, and lemon zest in another medium bowl, and then fold in the whipped cream. (The cream can be prepared 1 day ahead; cover and refrigerate. Whisk gently for a few seconds when ready to use.)

MAKES 2 CUPS

 NOTE: Robertson's lemon curd is widely available and works well in this recipe.

Whipped Maple Cream

Softly whipped cream takes on a whole new persona when combined with maple syrup and sour cream. The sweetness of the syrup balanced by the slightly acidic touch of sour cream produces a simple yet stunningly flavored sauce. Try it on Pumpkin Waffles (page 29), Multigrain Extravaganza Waffles (page 23), or Waffled French Toasts (page 34).

½ cup heavy (whipping) cream
½ cup sour cream
¼ cup pure maple syrup

➤ With an electric mixer on medium-high speed, whip the cream in a medium bowl until firm. Fold in the sour cream, then gently whisk in the maple syrup. (The cream can be prepared 1 day ahead; cover and refrigerate. Whisk gently for a few seconds when ready to use.)

MAKES 1½ CUPS

Spiced Honey Whipped Cream

The secret to the great flavor of this whipped cream lies in its beautifully balanced sweet and tart tastes. Honey and ground coriander provide the sweetness, while sour cream contributes a slightly tart note to softly whipped cream. This topping is exceptionally good on Whole Wheat Waffles (page 21), Pumpkin Waffles (page 29), or Holiday Waffles (page 32).

½ cup heavy (whipping) cream
2 tablespoons honey
½ teaspoon ground coriander
½ cup sour cream
Ground cinnamon for garnish

➤ With an electric mixer on medium-high speed, whip the cream in a medium bowl until soft peaks form. Reduce the speed to low and add the honey and coriander. Continue whipping until stiff peaks form. With a wire whisk, fold in the sour cream. This will deflate the stiffly whipped cream slightly, giving it a yogurt-like consistency. (The cream can be prepared 1 day ahead; cover and refrigerate. Whisk gently for a few seconds when ready to use.)

➤ Serve the cream in a bowl and dust it with cinnamon.

MAKES ABOUT 1½ CUPS

Whipped Mascarpone Cream

Nothing could be simpler to prepare than this special topping made with only three ingredients. Mascarpone, an extra-rich Italian cream cheese, adds a slight hint of acidity to softly whipped cream, while honey provides a sweet accent. This sweet garnish is particularly tempting paired with Going Nuts Waffles (page 64) or as an embellishment along with fresh strawberries for Raised Belgian Waffles (page 57).

1 cup heavy (whipping) cream
6 tablespoons mascarpone cheese
4 teaspoons honey

➤ With an electric mixer on medium-high speed, whip the cream in a medium bowl until it just starts to thicken. Reduce the speed to medium and beat in the mascarpone and honey. Continue beating until the cream is firm, a few seconds more. (The cream can be prepared 3 hours ahead; cover and refrigerate. Whisk gently for a few seconds when ready to use.)

MAKES ABOUT 2 CUPS

Fruit Compotes, Salsas, and Chutneys

Apricot-Cherry Compote

The dried apricots and cherries in this compote look like glistening jewels after slowly simmering in a spiced sugar syrup. Toasted walnuts add a crunchy accent to the warm fruits. Pair the compote with hearty choices, such as Gingerbread Waffles (page 58), Pumpkin Waffles (page 29), or Whole Wheat Waffles (page 21).

10 ounces (about 1¼ cups) dried apricots, halved
1 cup boiling water
¾ cup freshly squeezed orange juice
½ cup sugar
¾ teaspoon ground ginger
One 3-inch cinnamon stick, broken in half
⅔ cup dried cherries
⅓ cup dry white wine
⅓ cup coarsely chopped toasted walnuts (see Note page 29)

➤ Put the apricots in a medium heat-proof bowl and pour the boiling water over them. Let them soften for 10 minutes, then drain and reserve the apricots.

➤ Combine ¾ cup water, the orange juice, sugar, ginger, and cinnamon stick halves in a medium saucepan set over medium heat. Stir until the sugar dissolves. Reduce the heat to low and simmer 5 minutes.

➤ Add the apricots, cherries, and wine to the pan. Cook until the fruits are glazed and tender, and most of the liquids have evaporated, 10 minutes or longer. Remove and discard the cinnamon halves. Stir in the walnuts. (The compote can be prepared 2 days ahead; cool, cover, and refrigerate. Reheat, stirring, over low heat.)

MAKES ABOUT 2½ CUPS

Apple-Raisin Compote

For this satisfying fruit topping, sliced Golden Delicious apples are sautéed until tender in both brown and white sugars along with fragrant spices, then combined with rum-soaked raisins. This compote, which can be cooked a day ahead, makes an especially scrumptious garnish to Whole Wheat Waffles (page 21), Multigrain Extravaganza Waffles (page 23), or Waffled French Toasts (page 34). Simply spoon the warm apple slices and their pan juices over the waffles, and for an extra special touch, garnish with dollops of Whipped Maple Cream (page 84).

3 tablespoons dark rum
⅓ cup raisins
5 to 6 Golden Delicious apples
¾ cup granulated sugar
¾ cup packed light brown sugar
¼ cup all-purpose flour
1 teaspoon ground cinnamon
½ teaspoon freshly grated nutmeg
1 tablespoon unsalted butter, diced
⅓ cup chopped toasted walnut halves (see Note page 29)

➤ Heat the rum in a small, heavy saucepan over medium heat a few seconds, until just barely warm. (Do not heat until hot or the rum will flame.) Remove the pan from the heat and stir in the raisins. Set aside.

➤ Peel, core, and halve the apples lengthwise. Cut the halves into ¼-inch-thick slices to yield 6 cups. (Save extra apples for another use.)

➤ In a large, heavy skillet, mix together the sugars, flour, cinnamon, and nutmeg with a spoon until well blended. Add the apple slices and toss to coat well. Add the butter. Place the pan over medium heat and cook, stirring constantly until the sugar dissolves and the apples begin to release their juices, 4 to 5 minutes. Reduce the heat to medium-low and continue to cook, stirring frequently, until the apples are soft but not mushy and the juices have thickened, about 10 minutes.

➤ Remove the skillet from the heat and stir the raisins, any rum in the saucepan, and the walnuts into the skillet. (The compote can be prepared 1 day ahead; cool, cover, and refrigerate. Reheat, stirring, over low heat.)

MAKES 3 CUPS

Cranberry-Apple Compote

Cranberries and apples are the starring duo in this compote. The fruits are sautéed in butter, then simmered in cider scented with cinnamon. This colorful topping, which can be prepared in advance, makes an impressive garnish to use during the holidays. Try it as a partner to Holiday Waffles (page 32), Waffled French Toasts (page 34), or Multigrain Extravaganza Waffles (page 23).

2 cups apple cider
6 tablespoons light corn syrup
2 tablespoons packed light brown sugar
Two 3-inch cinnamon sticks, broken in half
8 tablespoons (1 stick) unsalted butter, divided
3 medium Golden Delicious apples
2 cups fresh or frozen cranberries
½ cup granulated sugar, plus more if needed

➤ Whisk together the cider, corn syrup, and brown sugar in a large, wide saucepan. Add the cinnamon stick halves and place the saucepan over high heat. Bring the cider mixture to a strong simmer and continue to cook, whisking occasionally, until the mixture has reduced by half, to 1 cup, 15 to 20 minutes or more. Whisk in half of the butter until melted. Remove and set aside.

➤ Peel, quarter, and core the apples; cut the quarters into ½-inch pieces. Melt the remaining butter in a large, heavy skillet over medium heat until hot. Sauté the apples, stirring for 2 minutes, then add the cranberries and granulated sugar. Stir constantly until the cranberries begin to pop, about 2 minutes. Add the reduced cider mixture and raise the heat to high. Cook until the mixture becomes thick and syrupy, about 5 minutes.

➤ Remove the pan from the heat and discard the cinnamon halves. Taste and add 1 to 2 tablespoons granulated sugar, if desired. (The compote can be prepared 1 day ahead; cool, cover, and refrigerate. Reheat, stirring, over medium heat.)

MAKES ABOUT 3 CUPS

Avocado Salsa

Velvety-smooth bits of avocado, sweet diced grape tomatoes, and chopped red onion form the basis of this vibrant salsa. Tossed in fresh lime juice and seasoned with lime zest and cilantro, this garnish is especially good with Southwest Waffles (page 51) or Corn Waffles (page 49).

2 ripe, but not mushy, avocados, peeled and cut into ½-inch dice
1 cup grape tomatoes, diced
¼ cup chopped red onion
¼ cup chopped fresh cilantro
2 tablespoons plus 2 teaspoons freshly squeezed lime juice
1 teaspoon grated lime zest
½ teaspoon kosher salt, plus more if needed
3 bacon strips, fried and crumbled for garnish (optional)

➤ In a medium, nonreactive bowl, combine all the ingredients except the bacon, tossing gently. Taste and add more salt, if desired. (The salsa can be prepared 4 hours ahead; cover and refrigerate. Bring it to room temperature 30 minutes before using.) If desired, sprinkle the salsa with crumbled bacon when ready to serve.

MAKES 2½ TO 3 CUPS

Orange Ambrosia

This topping with tropical accents is delicious when paired with softly whipped cream as a garnish to Coconut Waffles (page 62), or as a nontraditional embellishment for Raised Belgian Waffles (page 57). It's also a winning partner with Multigrain Extravaganza Waffles (page 23).

4 large navel oranges
2 to 3 teaspoons orange liqueur, such as Grand Marnier
½ cup toasted sweetened coconut flakes (see Note page 62)
⅓ cup toasted sliced almonds (see Note page 29)

➤ Peel the oranges, removing the skin and all of the white membranes beneath. With a sharp knife, cut out the orange segments and remove and discard any seeds. Cut the segments into ½-inch pieces and put them in a medium bowl with the orange liqueur. Stir to mix. (The fruit can be prepared 3 hours ahead; cover and refrigerate.)

➤ To serve, add the coconut flakes and almonds to the bowl and toss.

MAKES ABOUT 2½ CUPS

Tomato and Yellow Pepper Salsa

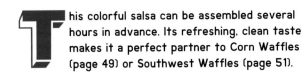

his colorful salsa can be assembled several hours in advance. Its refreshing, clean taste makes it a perfect partner to Corn Waffles (page 49) or Southwest Waffles (page 51).

2 cups (about 1 pound) seeded and diced tomatoes
⅔ cup (about 1 medium) diced yellow bell pepper
½ cup chopped red onion
¼ cup chopped fresh cilantro
2 tablespoons (2 to 3) minced jalapeño chiles
   (see Note)
2 tablespoons plus 2 teaspoons freshly squeezed lime
   juice
4 teaspoons olive oil
1 teaspoon salt, plus more if needed

➤ In a medium nonreactive bowl, combine all the ingredients, tossing gently. Taste and add more salt, if desired. (The salsa can be prepared 4 hours ahead; cover and refrigerate. Bring it to room temperature 30 minutes before using.)

MAKES ABOUT 3 CUPS

NOTE: The tissues around your mouth, nose, and eyes are very sensitive to the oils of hot chiles, so if you touch any of these areas with chile-coated fingers, you will feel an unpleasant burning sensation! Wearing rubber gloves when seeding and chopping chiles will prevent this problem. Remove the gloves and wash them as soon as you are finished.

Plum Chutney

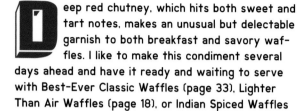eep red chutney, which hits both sweet and tart notes, makes an unusual but delectable garnish to both breakfast and savory waffles. I like to make this condiment several days ahead and have it ready and waiting to serve with Best-Ever Classic Waffles (page 33), Lighter Than Air Waffles (page 18), or Indian Spiced Waffles (page 44)

1 pound (about 4) red plums
⅓ cup sugar
⅓ cup packed light brown sugar
6 tablespoons cider vinegar
1 tablespoon chopped peeled fresh ginger
½ teaspoon ground cardamom
One 3-inch cinnamon stick, broken in half

➤ Halve the plums and remove and discard the pits. Cut the halves into ½-inch dice.

➤ Put 1 cup water and both sugars in a medium saucepan over medium-high heat. Stir just until the sugar dissolves, then bring the mixture to a boil without stirring. Add half of the plums, the vinegar, ginger, cardamom, and cinnamon stick halves, and cook for 5 minutes. Add the remaining plums and cook until the mixture has thickened and is syrupy, 8 to 10 minutes more. Carefully, with a spoon, remove the cinnamon halves and discard.

➤ (The chutney can be prepared 5 days ahead; cool, cover and refrigerate. Reheat, stirring, over low heat.) Serve warm.

MAKES ABOUT 1½ CUPS

Waffles and Toppings

Waffles	Apple-Raisin Compote	Apricot-Cherry Compote	Avocado Salsa	Cider Syrup	Cranberry-Apple Compote	Cranberry Syrup	Dark Chocolate Sauce	Extra-Rich Caramel Sauce	Lemon Chantilly Cream	Maple-Pecan Syrup	Night Before Blueberry Sauce	Orange Ambrosia	Orange-Honey Butter	Orange-Scented Whipped Cream	Pecan Toffee Crunch Butter	Plum Chutney	Smooth as Silk Raspberry Glaze	Spiced Honey Whipped Cream	Summertime Strawberry Sauce	Tomato and Yellow Pepper Salsa	Warm Lemon Sauce	Whipped Maple Cream	Whipped Mascarpone Cream
Banana Waffles								✳		✳													✳
Bananas Foster Waffles								✳															
Best-Ever Classic Waffles	✳	✳		✳	✳	✳				✳	✳		✳	✳	✳	✳			✳				
Buttermilk Waffles	✳	✳		✳	✳	✳				✳	✳		✳	✳	✳	✳			✳				
Chocolate Chip–Pecan Waffles							✳	✳						✳									✳
Chocolate Waffles							✳	✳						✳									✳
Coconut Waffles							✳					✳											
Corn Waffles			✳																	✳			
Double Blueberry Waffles									✳		✳											✳	
Ginger Waffles																✳							
Gingerbread Waffles	✳	✳								✳								✳				✳	✳
Going Nuts Waffles													✳	✳									✳
Holiday Waffles					✳	✳							✳					✳					✳
Lemon Poppy Seed Waffles									✳		✳										✳		
Lighter Than Air Waffles	✳	✳		✳	✳	✳				✳	✳		✳	✳	✳	✳			✳				
Multigrain Extravaganza Waffles	✳	✳		✳	✳					✳	✳	✳	✳	✳								✳	
Pizzelle							✳																
Pizzelle Ice Cream Sandwiches							✳																
Pumpkin Waffles		✳		✳						✳						✳		✳				✳	
Raised Belgian Waffles		✳			✳	✳				✳	✳	✳	✳	✳				✳	✳				✳
Southwest Waffles			✳																	✳			
Very Berry Waffles									✳		✳			✳				✳			✳		
Waffle Trifle																		✳					
Waffled French Toasts	✳			✳	✳	✳				✳	✳		✳					✳				✳	
Warm Waffle "Bread" Pudding								✳															
Whole Wheat Waffles	✳	✳		✳	✳					✳			✳		✳			✳				✳	

For Cornbread Waffles, Crisp Waffles with Sausages, Croque-Monsieur Waffles, Herbed Waffles, Orange Waffles, Sour Cream Waffles, and Waffles Benedict, see individual recipes.

Index

Table of Equivalents

The exact equivalents in the following tables have been rounded for convenience.

LIQUID/DRY MEASURES

U.S.	METRIC
¼ teaspoon	1.25 milliliters
½ teaspoon	2.5 milliliters
1 teaspoon	5 milliliters
1 tablespoon (3 teaspoons)	15 milliliters
1 fluid ounce (2 tablespoons)	30 milliliters
¼ cup	60 milliliters
⅓ cup	80 milliliters
½ cup	120 milliliters
1 cup	240 milliliters
1 pint (2 cups)	480 milliliters
1 quart (4 cups, 32 ounces)	960 milliliters
1 gallon (4 quarts)	3.84 liters
1 ounce (by weight)	28 grams
1 pound	454 grams
2.2 pounds	1 kilogram

OVEN TEMPERATURE

FAHRENHEIT	CELSIUS	GAS
250	120	½
275	140	1
300	150	2
325	160	3
350	180	4
375	190	5
400	200	6
425	220	7
450	230	8
475	240	9
500	260	10

LENGTH

U.S.	METRIC
⅛ inch	3 millimeters
¼ inch	6 millimeters
½ inch	12 millimeters
1 inch	2.5 centimeters